HARVEY KEITEL

MOVIE TOP TEN

CREDITS

HARVEY KEITEL: MOVIE TOP TEN
Edited by Jack Hunter
ISBN 1 871592 87 9
A Butcherbest Production
© Creation Books & individual contributors 1999
Creation Movie Top Tens: a periodical, review-based publication
First published 1999 by:
Creation Books International
Design/layout/typesetting:
Bradley Davis, PCP International
Cover illustration:
"Reservoir Dogs"

Photo credits:
All photos by courtesy of the BFI, London; Museum Of Modern Art, New York; and the Jack Hunter Collection.

British Library Cataloguing in Publication Data:
A catalogue record for this book is available from the British Library

Editor's acknowledgements
Thanks to: All the contributors, in particular Jack Sargeant, Mikita Brottman and Chris Campion.

Creation Books
"Popular books for popular people"

CONTENTS

INTRODUCTION
"PROMISE, OBLIVION, STARDOM"

"Disturbance" is a word that crops up repeatedly when Harvey Keitel tries to identify the source of his motivation to act. Disturbance of the psyche. Disturbance of the equilibrium. Disturbance of emotions. These are things that Keitel conjures up in performances which have run a gamut of polarised personas: good cop, bad cop, gangster, pimp, lover, father, street thug, working man. What Keitel brings is a meticulous eye for detail and depth of character that digs under the surface of archetypal roles often reduced to crude stereotypes in the hands of others. He carries with him a primal emotional power and honesty and a feral presence that dominates the screen.

But Keitel's three decade career has also been one long battle. On one level for recognition as a working actor with a sense of purpose in the films he chooses to make, on another for the control of his soul. "Hopefully by understanding [the] disturbance, we can start a dialogue with other people," he has said[1]. Writer-director James Toback succinctly described Keitel's career path in terms of the mythical three-act structure so beloved of Hollywood: "from promise to oblivion to stardom"[2]. Keitel frequently describes his body of work as a journey.

"There's a great deal of pain and pleasure I'm getting from this journey," he admitted, "from searching for this disturbance, coming to grips with it and discovering my own true nature. I understand the disturbance now, at great cost. And it's a price worthwhile paying. Disturbance takes on different natures as you go through it. Make no mistake. It doesn't happen in one flash. In one's disturbance, there's everything. There is rage. There is loneliness. Happiness."[3]

Keitel's journey began in earnest in on May 13, 1939 in Brighton Beach, Brooklyn when he was born to lower-middle-class, orthodox Jewish, immigrant parents. As an adolescent, he battled with his parents and veered into juvenile delinquency, adopting the '50s teen uniform of black leather jacket, "duck's-ass" haircut, peg pants and pointy shoes. But his notions of toughness were redefined by seeing James Dean and Marlon Brando on the silver screen. "I related to James Dean," he recalled, "because he was in situations that we were in. I never related to his tough guy side. It was always his sensitivity and yet that was exactly what I couldn't be. I always buried it."[4]

Preferring the pool hall to the class room, he flunked out of school at seventeen. Finding himself broke and unemployed with few prospects, he decided to better himself by joining the military and enroled in the marines. One night, while practising night manoeuvres at the North Carolina camp he had been posted to, something happened that affected his outlook on life. Sitting outside in pitch blackness, armed for combat and scared to death, Keitel supposedly heard his drill instructor's voice say, "You're all afraid of the dark, because you're all afraid of what you don't know. I'm going to teach you to know the darkness so that you're no longer afraid of it. So that you learn how to live in it." These words would remain with Keitel and become a credo for his art.[5]

On the boat back to the US, after six months of active peace-keeping service in the Lebanon, Keitel started reading a book of Greek mythology, the continuing study of which (in addition to a growing interest in philosophy and religion) would prove to be the basis of his belief in his life and art as a journey. "I had a desire to understand the chaos that I was experiencing in my body," he explained. "And books were a guide."[6]

Returning to Brooklyn in 1965, after three years in the marines, Keitel got a job first as a shoe salesman then as a court stenographer. It was a trade he would ply for eight years while taking classes at Stella Adler's School Of Acting, which he started in 1962 at the suggestion from a work colleague. It soon became clear to Keitel that, in acting, he had finally found a way to express himself and get in touch with facets of his personality that he was struggling to understand.

PROMISE

In 1965, answering an ad in a trade paper seeking actors for a student project, Keitel came face to face for the first time with a hyperactive, fast-talking Italian-American called Martin Scorsese. Their connection on an intellectual level was almost instantaneous and Scorsese decided the young, inexperienced actor was right for the lead in his film, **Who's That Knocking At My Door?**, which was based on Scorsese's experiences as a young man growing up in Little Italy. The film was completed after three years work (during which Keitel still worked as a stenographer by day); it received good notices, and enjoyed a brief theatrical run before fading into obscurity to the disappointment of all involved.

But Keitel now had the acting bug and quit his job to pursue his new career full-time, taking freelance stenography work only when debt dictated. He took to the stage until Scorsese came knocking again in 1972, this time with funding to make **Mean Streets**, another film set on the streets of Little Italy. Keitel played Charlie Cappa, one of two hoodlums, opposite Robert De Niro. But although Cappa was the film's central figure, De Niro's portrayal of the itchy-fingered Johnny Boy stole the plaudits and, post **Mean Streets**, while De Niro's career soared (with an Oscar-winning role in Francis Ford Coppola's **The Godfather II**), Keitel's slumped. He took work wherever he could get it (including playing a generic thug on *Kojak*).

Scorsese came to his rescue again. After landing a gig directing **Alice Doesn't Live Here Any More**, he convinced Warners to let him cast Keitel as Ben, a man caught up in turmoil between his family and his lover. Such was his emotional involvement in the scene where he confronts his wife that Keitel went wild, put his fist through a glass door and scared the hell out of everyone on set.

After **Alice** it was back to TV movies and theatre productions (including a stint on Broadway in Arthur Miller's *Death Of A Salesman*), until Warners green-lighted **Taxi Driver** in 1975. Scorsese offered Keitel the role of the campaign organiser (eventually played by Albert Brooks). To Scorsese's surprise the actor chose to play Jodie Foster's pimp, Sport.

Working from the description "Italian guy standing in the doorway" of a four-line part in the original script, Keitel created a fully-rounded character symbolising Travis Bickle's shadow and nemesis. He based Sport on real pimps he saw in and around the Hell's Kitchen neighbourhood he lived in. He even approached one of them to rehearse with them, spent hours discussing the ins and outs of the pimp game and improvising scenes with Keitel playing the hooker to the pimp and vice versa.

The critical and commercial success of **Taxi Driver** eased the path into films like Robert Altman's **Buffalo Bill And The Indians** (1976) and Alan Rudolph's **Welcome To LA** (1977), and a starring role in Peter Yates' farcical **Mother, Jugs And Speed** (1976) opposite Rachel Welch and Bill Cosby.

OBLIVION

In 1976, Keitel was given his biggest break so far, but it was also to prove to the curse of his career. Francis Ford Coppola cast him as Sgt. Willard, the lead in **Apocalypse Now**, opposite one of his idols, Marlon Brando. It was a film innately connected to Keitel's history; his service in the marines and the impact that the Vietnam War had on his understanding of the world.

"I began by supporting the war," he said recently[7]. "As the years went by, and I had many conversations, debates and arguments with fellow actors, writers and directors – culminating in my reading Senator Fulbright's book *The Arrogance Of Power* – I got turned around about the Vietnam War and became a protester. Then that aphorism that many were so fond of saying, 'My country right or wrong', took on new meaning. I realised what does that mean? If my country is wrong don't I have a responsibility to say so."

In accepting the part in **Apocalypse Now** (which had been turned down by no less than McQueen, Redford, Nicholson and Pacino), Keitel dearly wanted to make a difference in his country's perception of the Vietnam War.

The Duellists

Initially, he felt that Coppola's aim was the same. But when the shoot decamped to the Philippines for the start of a gruelling six month shoot, things quickly began to unravel.

Unhappy that Coppola lorded it in a lavish villa while the actors were housed in barracks, Keitel's unease was compounded by his inability to connect with the director, who seemed more concerned with shooting schedules and budgets than his character's motivation. Things came to a head over Coppola's decision to shut down the set so that Brando could have time off to visit his children during the summer. This meant extending the shoot to conflict with that of another film Keitel had already agreed to make. Coppola was also trying to sign the actor to a seven-year contract with his Zoetrope Studios. In negotiations, Keitel dug his heels in and was unceremoniously fired, the role then going to Martin Sheen. The notice appeared on the front page of *Variety* – headline: "Keitel Fired, Won't Wait For Brando" – establishing his "reputation" as a "difficult" actor for years to come. "Had I known then what I know now, I would have kept my mouth shut longer and had them shoot so much they couldn't fire me," Keitel would comment later.

Amazingly, after this knockback, Keitel buried himself in work, completing three films in 1977 – Ridley Scott's **The Duellists**, James Toback's

Fingers and Paul Schrader's **Blue Collar** – which although critical and commercial failures at the time are now considered to contain some of his strongest performances. All were made with first-time directors willing to give Keitel the space and direction he needed to build. Keitel's role alongside (ironically) Martin Sheen in the quasi-mystical British Western **Eagle's Wing** (Anthony Harvey, 1978) confirmed his versatility.

According to an interview around the release of **Fingers**, it's obvious that by this stage Keitel was confident in his abilities, having honed a technique based on what he had learned at Stella Adler that enabled him to physically and emotionally embody his character. "You get the script and you analyse it," he said of his pre-shoot. "You dig into it, discover where the character is coming from, what his background is, what he does, what his desires are, what his fears are, how he lives – analysing what the author had in mind. And then, once the cameras roll, there is always that little something that is improvisational, spontaneous."

The continuing lack of commercial success all but killed his career in Hollywood for ten years. Instead he sought work in Europe, where his skills were more appreciated. But even then, financial necessity often forced him to choose work that degraded his abilities. At his absolute low-point in the early '80s, he took a role in an Italian mini-series called *Baciami Strega* (English translation: "Kiss Me Witch") and played the villain in the disastrous sci-fi thriller **Saturn 3** (1980), for which he suffered the ignominy of having his lines re-dubbed by another actor (with a British accent) in post-production. But there were also oddball projects that have since become cult movies – like **Deathwatch** (1980), Bertrand Tavernier's futuristic media fiction in which Keitel played a TV cameraman with video cameras for eyes; Nicolas Roeg's **Bad Timing** (1980); Robert Faenza's **Cop Killer** (1981); and James Toback's **Exposed** (1983), as a character based on Carlos The Jackal. In the mid-'80s, Keitel also acted on and off-Broadway in two well-received plays, David Rabe's *Hurly Burly* and Sam Shepherd's *A Lie Of The Mind*.

While his freefalling career may have frustrated him, his emotional life was fulfilled by his relationship with Lorraine Bracco, who he met and married in 1982. Their first child together, Stella, was born in 1985. Keitel's connections and support kick-started Bracco's acting career, landing her acclaimed roles in Toback's **The Pick-Up Artist**, Ridley Scott's **Someone To Watch Over Me** and Scorsese's **Goodfellas**.

STARDOM

In a cycle that dove-tails neatly with Keitel's internal search for resolution, the filmmakers he worked with early in their careers ended up returning the favour once they were established, helping to resurrect his reputation. The

Reservoir Dogs

first to offer a helping hand was Scorsese, who picked Keitel to play Judas in the Paul Schrader-scripted **Last Temptation Of Christ** (1988). Ridley Scott cast him as the sympathetic cop in **Thelma And Louise** (1991), the most successful studio picture Keitel had made for years. James Toback, who had become a close friend and confidante, scripted Barry Levinson's **Bugsy** (1991) – a film which won Keitel an Oscar-nomination for his portrayal of thuggish gangster, Mickey Cohen. He also played a corrupt estate agent, the foil to Jack Nicholson, in Nicholson's **Chinatown** sequel, **The Two Jakes** (1990).

But it was his involvement with Quentin Tarantino's **Reservoir Dogs** that assured Keitel's cult status throughout the '90s. After reading the script, passed to him by **Dogs'** producer Lawrence Bender's acting coach, Keitel used his clout to secure Tarantino a spot in the coveted Sundance scriptwriters conference. The finished film was the sensation of Sundance in 1992 and has since become a phenomenon. Keitel saw the film (in which he played clean-cut gangster, Mr. White) as a meditation on trust and betrayal – possibly because at this point in his life Bracco had just left him (for Edward James Olmos) and he was involved in a lengthy and recriminatory custody battle over their daughter.

The emotional trauma he was going through in real life poured out onto the screen in Abel Ferrara's unrepentant **Bad Lieutenant**. Keitel played

Smoke

the eponymous character as a man trapped in a personal hell, desperately seeking redemption. Themes of infidelity also surfaced in Ferrara's **Dangerous Game**, where Keitel played an intense art-house director who has an on-set affair with his leading lady (played by Madonna).

Now Keitel is a star, with all the power, prestige and status that confers. He flits between rounded (even light-hearted) cameos in studio flicks (including John Badham's **Point Of No Return** 1993, Barry Sonnenfeld's **Get Shorty** 1995, Tarantino's **Pulp Fiction** 1994, and Phil Kaufman's **Rising Sun** 1993); substantial roles that carry worthy art movies (such as his roles as the sensitive primitive Baines in Jane Campion's **The Piano** 1993, film-maker A— in Theo Angelopoulos' **Ulysses' Gaze** 1995, and cigar-shop owner Auggie Wren in Wayne Wang's **Smoke** 1995); and work with younger, happening directors (Spike Lee's **Clockers** 1995 and Robert Rodriguez's **From Dusk Till Dawn** 1996).

In 1997 he was able to reprise two of his more familiar characterisations, as a cop in James Mangold's big-budget **CopLand**, (alongside Robert De Niro and Stylvester Stallone), and as a heistman in John Irvin's more modest **City Of Industry**. This was the career path he had predicted for himself years earlier.

"I'm not interested in being a star if all that means is making money

Ulysses' Gaze

and having a name," he had said. "I want as much control as I can get, and I want to reach a bankable level only so that I can do the kind of work I want to do."

CODA

Sundance Film Festival 1999. Keitel is in town supporting a film by another young first-time director, Tony Bui's **Three Seasons**. The film (which went on to win the Sundance Dramatic Prize) is a fable set in modern-day Vietnam following the interlocking fates of four characters – a cyclo driver, a prostitute, a child cigarette vendor and a Vietnam veteran. Keitel plays the latter, a broken man looking for a daughter he has never known in order to bring meaning to his life. Such is Keitel's dedication to the movie that he has flown in for less than 24 hours, straight from the set of a movie he is making in Italy (**U-571**), a W.W.II submarine flick which he declines to talk about.

Jet-lagged and disorientated, he is wheeled around from one hotel suite to another on a round of press interviews. Keitel enters with a wry smile and graciously shakes the hands of the journalists present before taking a seat and mopping his brow. Tanned and healthy-looking, he sports an odd-looking pencil-thin moustache, wears a black leather jacket and trousers with a disingenuous leather travel pouch slung around his neck.

Keitel is notoriously evasive in interviews, revealing only what he wants to on his own terms. Motivation is dealt with only in broad sweeps of mythological and psychological parlance. But he speaks like a preacher, slowly but forcefully, determined to convince the congregation gathered before him of that which is right and good for the human spirit.

"Who among us has not experienced this need to find ourselves," he says. "That need to know more about our existence. A mythological need. Before, as a younger man, I wasn't thinking as clearly. It took a journey for me to make it clear who I was and what life is about."

NOTES

1. Interview with Julian Schnabel, "Jake Jake: Jack Nicholson & Harvey Keitel" (*Interview*, Vol.20, No. 8, p.90).

2. Marshall Fine, "Harvey Keitel: The Art Of Darkness", p.215.

3. Interview with Julian Schnabel, "Jake Jake: Jack Nicholson & Harvey Keitel" (*Interview*, Vol.20, No. 8, p.92).

4. Marshall Fine, "Harvey Keitel: The Art Of Darkness", p.18.

5. Marshall Fine, "Harvey Keitel: The Art Of Darkness", p.29.

6. Marshall Fine, "Harvey Keitel: The Art Of Darkness", p.33–34.

7. Interview with the author at Sundance Film Festival, 1999.

"CRUEL MEN OF ROME": HONOUR & TRAGEDY IN 'MEAN STREETS'

THE PLAYERS

To the sound of the Ronettes singing "Be My Baby", the opening sequence of Martin Scorsese's **Mean Streets** (1973) presents us with a series of four short vignettes, each introducing us to one of "four honourable men", the major characters of the movie, in short scenes of their own.

A bar owner comes across a junkie shooting up in the john of his bar. Angrily, he throws both the junkie and his buddies out into the street. This, we are told, is Tony.

Making an illicit deal under some freeway overpass, a man in a smart black trenchcoat discovers he's just been ripped off. This man is Michael.

A third man in a pork-pie hat drops a parcel in a mailbox then moves quickly on down the street. The mailbox explodes behind him. This, we learn, is Johnny Boy.

A fourth man walks up to the altar in a Catholic Church, and kneels down to pray. This man is Charlie.

Tony, Michael, Johnny Boy and Charlie. "Four honourable men".

THE EMPIRE

The allusion to Julius Caesar is not accidental. **Mean Streets** is an episodic tragedy of character and destiny which plays itself out on a small stage – the New York empire of Little Italy, the neighbourhood of Mott, Mulberry and Elizabeth streets, the district in which Scorsese grew up. The narrative adheres to the classical unity of place – in this case, a small area comprising about ten square blocks of bars, movie theatres, Italian restaurants and Catholic churches in lower Manhattan. These "honourable men", a select group of small-time crooks, spend their days cruising the streets, closing deals, drinking at Tony's place, chasing girls, getting into fights and going to watch John Wayne movies. Tony (David Proval) is a low-profile proprietor, owner of a sleazy establishment with black strippers and regular fights. The patrician Michael (played by the aptly named Richard Romanus) is a smooth but violent loan shark who takes his business very seriously indeed.

The head of the Roman Empire, the reigning Caesar, is Charlie's Uncle Giovanni (played by the equally aptly named Cesare Danova), the neighbourhood Mafia don. Charlie (Harvey Keitel), who stands to inherit the

Caesar's robes, has the job of collecting payments for Uncle Giovanni, often from debtors who no longer have the means to pay him, such as Oscar, the proprietor of a once-prosperous Italian restaurant. Fortunately for Oscar, Giovanni has a generous streak, advising Charlie not to push for any more payments until Oscar's business picks up again. Giovanni, apparently, is also an "honourable man".

Mean Streets, described by *Rolling Stone* as "shocking, jolting, even pulverizing" and by the *New York Times* as "one of the finer American films", is the earliest of Scorsese's trademark movies, imbued with the urban nostalgia that would lead to such works as **Raging Bull** and **Taxi Driver**. It introduces his identifying themes of Catholic guilt, misguided loyalties and small-time gangster life with its insults and worries, the constant chasing after minor debts and deals, always on the edge of any major action. These men are neighbours, low-level hoods, hustlers, showmen, and not real mobsters.

The film is also a virtuoso performance of technical effects. As in **Taxi Driver**, the scene is shot sometimes from above, sometimes from below, and a hand-held camera is used for the more dynamic scenes. Smoothly paced and balanced, the film is cut and scored with great skill. Sharp editing ensures maximum visual impact, backed up by a memorable soundtrack which mixes Italian opera and '60s rock with great flair. Most impressive of all, perhaps, is the tone of the film, its creative use of colour, over-exposed almost to monochrome in the street sequences, then saturated deep into the red for scenes such as the following one, set in Tony's bar.

Michael is standing by the jukebox, picking out records. A young girl comes up to him and puts her hand on his back.

"Michael, play all the old ones. Old ones," she begs him.

Michael makes his selection and puts his coin in the slot. A record comes on. It is "Oldies But Goodies", by Little Caesar and the Romans.

THE HERO AND HIS LOYALTIES

In one of the defining roles of his career, Harvey Keitel oscillates between convivial generosity, violent cynicism and naive vulnerability in his role as Charlie, the empire's Mark Antony figure. Charlie is torn between his own ambitious loyalty to the family and the family business, and his friendship with the endearing but self-destructive Johnny Boy (Robert de Niro), a fighter and a hustler, cocky and abrasive, an unstable ne'er-do-well, an angel of anarchy, always acting up. Dissolute, irresponsible, he dances on the stage with strippers, owes money to everybody, hustles pool, and is always getting himself and others involved in huge bar-room brawls.

The epithet "honourable" is never used of Johnny Boy without a sarcastic edge to it, as thought intended to mock and berate him for the

qualities he so obviously lacks, in much the same way as the word is used by Mark Antony of the conspirators in Julius Caesar. And Johnny Boy's suicidal trigger-happiness, his reckless arrogance in the face of death, echoes the thoughts of Julius Caesar, that "it seems to me most strange that men should fear, Seeing that death, a necessary end, Will come when it will come".

Charlie's love for Johnny Boy is his tragic flaw, effecting the turn in his fortunes and, ultimately, the loss of his life. Like all great tragedies, **Mean Streets** follows the path of a hero, but a flawed hero, charting his inevitable decline, the result of his inability to overcome this one, single failing. Like Mark Antony torn between his "gaudy nights" with Cleopatra and his official duties as leader of the Roman Empire, Charlie is divided by his love for Johnny and his loyalty to his uncle and the rest of the Family. His affection for Johnny Boy is severely frowned upon by Giovanni and the other gangland leaders, who regard it as a weakness, a distraction, Charlie's Achilles Heel. But – again, like Antony with Cleopatra – this is the defining relationship of Charlie's life, one that he feels unable to sacrifice, no matter how great the cost. Johnny Boy is both his fortune and his failure, his surrogate child and his alter ego, his counterpart from the world of shadows. Like Antony, he forsakes his duties to the empire for the sake of his duties to his *compagnero*, and, also like Antony, ends up paying a severe price for what, in the eyes of the Empire at least, is seen as keenly misguided loyalty.

The real trouble starts when Johnny starts to default on his payments to Michael. Michael is a ruling member of the Empire and the family, and Johnny Boy is an outsider, a trickster, a playboy, and a hustler. By vouching for Johnny with Michael, Charlie has found himself in a no-win situation. But his loyalty to his friend remains strong. Michael can't understand why Charlie would jeopardize his future by hanging out with a breezy character like Johnny Boy.

"I can't explain Johnny," replies Charlie.

His explanation is no less frank than that of Antony, who, when questioned about his relationship with Caesar, describes himself simply as "a plain, blunt man that loves my friend".

THE HERO AND HIS HONOUR

While Johnny Boy prances around on the stage at Tony's place with the strippers and Charlie watches him, drinking with a shaky hand, the audience is given access to an interior monologue, a soliloquy of sorts, revealing some of Charlie's complicated meditations on the nature of penance. Charlie is a Catholic, though of a somewhat unorthodox nature. He reconciles his religious beliefs with his day-to-day sinning through his conviction that penance takes place on the streets, not in the church. "I do my own penance for my own sins," he concludes to himself. To Charlie, good and evil, sin and salvation are matters of the street, and not of the soul. He accepts his fortune as heir to the gritty kingdom, but seeks nonetheless to perform an act of redemption as a means of earning it. Somehow, in some way, he seems to believe that his protective devotion to Johnny plays a significant part in his self-styled penance.

On the streets of Little Italy, Mark Antony merges with Saint Anthony; the narrative, also adhering to the classical unity of time, is set around the great feast of Saint Anthony, the main Catholic festival of the Italian neighbourhood. Like the eponymous Bad Lieutenant in Abel Ferrara's film, Charlie's struggle with Catholicism is personal, sometimes bitter, and always painful. The other men mock his faith, calling him "Saint Charles", going down on their knees and blessing him in mockery when he walks into the bar ("hey hey hey everybody, Saint Charles is here! Benediction!"), and yet – again, like the Bad Lieutenant – Charlie has few qualms about drinking, fighting, gambling, ripping people off and consorting with prostitutes. Like Mark Antony, Charlie is a hero, but a flawed hero, apparently determined to make life as tough as possible for himself, a trial to endure, especially in his destructive defense of the reckless Johnny Boy. Just as he does in **Bad Lieutenant**, Keitel in **Mean Streets** delivers a blisteringly authentic performance as a man torn between conflicting loyalties, beset by demons on all sides.

Unlike the Bad Lieutenant, however, Charlie seems to have a genuinely tender side to his nature. When Tony shows the guys his pet lion cub, Charlie gazes at the animal in fondness and awe ("hey Tony, it's beautiful," he says affectionately). Nowhere is this tender side to his nature made clearer than in his relationship with Johnny Boy, with whom he hides from debtors, roughhouses, fights with garbage-pail lids, jokes about family and priests. And though Johnny may be treacherous in every other way, in friendship he is ardent and devoted. Charlie might well echo Mark Antony's words about Caesar, that despite all his other shortcomings, "He was my friend, faithful and just to me".

In one scene, Johnny stays overnight at Charlie's place and sleeps with Charlie in his bed, beneath a single crucifix. "Did you say your prayers?" Charlie asks him. "Very funny," says Johnny Boy. "Hey, why don't you come over here and tuck me in, sweetheart?"

We also witness this gentle, tender side to Charlie's character in a scene when a buddy just back from Vietnam goes berserk and shoots up Tony's bar. Charlie rescues a young girl in the back room, puts his arms around her and slow-dances with her gently, like Sport with Iris in **Taxi Driver**, until she passes out on his shoulder. He then lays her considerately down on a sofa and covers her body thoughtfully with a blanket. This gentle side to his character also means he's a little too soft on his Uncle Giovanni's debtors, disposed to letting situations get out of hand rather than nipping them in the bud.

THE TRAGIC FLAW

Johnny Boy's cousin Teresa (Amy Robinson), with whom Charlie is having a clandestine affair, is also irritated by Charlie's seemingly irrational loyalty to the errant trickster. "I don't know why you hang round with Johnny," she complains. "He's like an insane person."

"You've got to help people," Charlie responds, with conviction. "Johnny's just a kid who... needs to be helped... Saint Francis of Assisi had it all down. People should help other people first."

"Bullshit," replies Teresa. "Saint Francis of Assisi didn't run numbers. You should help yourself first."

Charlie's relationship with Teresa is poignant evidence of his transparent envy of "ordinary" people, people who live "normal" lives, people who don't live on the streets. He's the only one of the "honourable men" to express disillusion with their lifestyle, to confess that hanging out in Tony's dark bar is making him depressed. He may not enjoy the outdoor life, but he has his tastes. "I hate the sun, I hate the beach, I hate the ocean, I

hate the heat," he complains cynically to Teresa during a walk on the beach.

"Charlie, what *do* you like?" she asks him.

His face lights up with an expression that is vulnerable, naive, almost angelic. "I like spaghetti with clam sauce ...I like John Wayne," he tells her, "and I like you."

Charlie's ambition, which he describes with open eyes and a nearly enchanted countenance, is to open up a place of his own, an Italian restaurant, somewhere uptown. When Uncle Giovanni and his fellow patricians talk money and politics at their table at Oscar's place, Charlie wanders into the restaurant kitchens, fascinated, compelled, joking with the chefs, intrigued by the different ovens and the various workings of the kitchen. When he returns to the table, Uncle Giovanni confronts him. "You're still around that kid, Johnny Boy," he says. "Honourable men go with honourable men... He's half-crazy..."

His uncle's highborn cynicism urges Charlie to reconsider the dangerous symbiosis of his relationship with Johnny Boy, prompting one last-ditch attempt to get Johnny back on the straight and narrow. "Hey, you go back to work tomorrow Johnny, or I'm gonna break both your arms, we understand each other?" he tells his prankster friend affectionately that night. Like Mark Antony on the battlefield, Charlie has realized that "There is a tide

in the affairs of men, which, taken at the flood, leads on to fortune... And we must take the current when it serves, Or lose our ventures". Charlie's venture is his restaurant. His relationship with Johnny Boy, like Antony's with Cleopatra, is hindering the fulfilment of his venture, and the fruition of his dreams.

In this light, it seems significant that both Charlie and Johnny Boy share a fondness for John Wayne movies, and in one scene, in which they visit a movie theatre, we see a very brief glimpse of the film they've chosen to see – John Ford's classic western, **The Searchers**. An epic quest set in and around Monument Valley, **The Searchers** is one of Scorsese's favourite films, one which strongly influenced him as a child, and a film whose narrative structure provides the basis for his later film, **Taxi Driver**.

Ethan Edwards, the John Wayne character in **The Searchers**, is a lawless wanderer with an abiding horror of miscegenation. This aversion is so intense that, when he finally discovers the niece he's spent so many years searching for (played by Natalie Wood), he's ready to shoot her on sight simply because she's been made one of the wives of an Indian chief. In some ways, Charlie in **Mean Streets** suffers from the same predicament, torn between his legitimate role as the successor to the family empire, and his fascination with the reviled "outsiders" to that family – Johnny Boy and his

sister, Teresa. His bitter sense of guilt at his love for Teresa cannot be assuaged, and when she expresses her affection for him he rejects her in a burst of aggressive, guilty denial:

> *Charlie:* Look, if there was any chance of me getting involved with you, I wouldn't be here right now, that's for sure.
> *Teresa:* Why not, Charlie?
> *Charlie:* Because you're a cunt, that's why.

STRUCTURE AND ORDER

Where Charlie is perhaps most similar to the Bad Lieutenant is in his compulsive need for rule and ritual, for prohibitions and regulations in a world without order. Like the Bad Lieutenant, his pursuit of discipline and ceremony returns him, inevitably, to the Catholic Church. And yet, to Charlie, the hidebound code of church order seems distant, and inappropriate for the life of the streets. Consequently, again like the Bad Lieutenant, Charlie finds solace in the artificial discipline and conformity of games.

Games have an order to them, a superlative kind of harmony that the rest of his life seems to be lacking. "I have come to create order," he says, mock-reverently, walking into Tony's place. He takes a glass of whisky and blesses it. Starting off playing a regular game of pool, he ends up subverting the rules drunkenly by shooting whisky glasses with his pool cue. He often carries round a deck of cards, and one of his characteristic tics is his continuous shuffling of the pack, always trying to persuade the others to play with him. "Hey, Tony, you want a game after the place closes?" he shouts, or "Michael, I have a game you cannot say no to." The game of friendship also has its code of conduct, which Charlie knows better than any of the others. He reprimands Johnny for beating up on Tony with the words "hey, c'mon, what the fuck is it with you guys, you're friends, remember?". His lovemaking with Teresa is also based around games of rules and rule-breaking; she asks him a number of times to cover his eyes while she dresses, and he cheats by peeking through the cracks in his fingers. Later on, he angers her by leaving her to go and meet Johnny Boy.

"Well, go and play your games with that dumb kid, I don't care," she tells him, finally.

"Teresa, it's no game," he responds, soberly.

Above all, the constant refrain of his ticing riff with Johnny Boy comprises a very peculiar and distinctive ritual in its own right:

Charlie: Whatsa madda wichoo?

Johnny Boy: Whaddya mean, whatsa madda with me? Whatsa madda wichoo?

Charlie: Whatsa madda with me? Nothing'sa madda with me. Whatsa madda wichoo?

THE TRAGEDY

Like his counterpart Mark Antony, Charlie is finally ripped apart and destroyed by the guilt of his torn loyalties. This sense of guilt is prevalent throughout the narrative, and foregrounded by the bristling scenes in which Charlie stands motionless before a mirror, confronting himself critically. It is also evidenced in the dream he recounts to Teresa, in which, on the verge of penetrating her, he comes blood all over her body.

Charlie's tragedy, like that of Mark Antony, is a shattering comeuppance that everyone but himself seems to see working its way to fruition. His fatal denouement, foreshadowed by dramatic Italian opera sung by Giuseppe de Stefano and Renato Carosone, is rooted in his inability to break off his friendship with Johnny Boy for the greater good – of the Family, of the Empire, of his own ambition. His alliance with the prankster is a lethal one, and lines him up against the ranks of Caesar. But it is the lordly Michael who finally proves to be his nemesis when, acting on behalf of Giovanni, he commits a drive-by shooting on the car in which Charlie, Teresa and Johnny

Boy are trying to leave town: "A Roman by a Roman valiantly vanquished".

In a final, elegiac vignette reminiscent of Charlie's dream, his car is shot off the road and careers into the side of a church, setting off a fire hydrant, which shoots up a spectacular jet of water all over the crashed car and the wrecked bodies inside it. Crawling out of the smashed ruins, Charlie dies on his knees, in prayer before the church, broken and bloodied. His death, like that of Mark Antony, is brave and noble "after the high Roman fashion", making death "proud to take" him. Water from the fire hydrant rains down on his prostrate body like holy water. Across the street, people close their blinds. Charlie lies dead on the ground, "none so poor to do him reverence". In the distance can be heard indistinct applause from some late night talk show being watched on television in someone's apartment.

'FINGERS'

"He has the hands of an artist and the mind of a madman" reads the tag-line of James Toback's **Fingers**, above a blood-red head-shot of a remorselessly staring Harvey Keitel superimposed over sheet music peppered with bullet holes. In this movie, music and murder, sex and madness are intertwined in the cloven psyche of its hero (as played by Keitel), Jimmy "Fingers" Angelelli, an aspiring concert pianist and reputedly the best debt collector in New York. He's a loner like Travis Bickle. A walking contradiction, gripping a tape deck in his left hand and wielding a gun in his right.

Jimmy may have chosen his nickname to acknowledge himself as a profligate musician, but it makes him sound like a petty gangster. The narrative is played out over the course of three days. Jimmy is immersed in his preparation for an piano recital audition at Carnegie Hall, in order to follow in the footsteps of his mother, Ruth (Marian Seldes) a former concert pianist. But he falls in love with a girl, Carol (Tia Farrow), who he believes has been brought to him by his music. She leads him into a sexual underworld inhabited by a pimp called Dreems (Jim Brown).

At the same time, Jimmy is given the task of collecting two debts for his father, Ben (Michael V. Gazzo), an ageing racketeer. The first one, from a pizza parlour owner, is simple enough, the second, from a bigger and badder mobster called Riccamonza (Anthony Sirico), proves to be a problem. The only way Jimmy can get Riccamonza's attention is by screwing his girlfriend in the bathroom of his health club. Invoking the mobster's wrath proves to be Jimmy's undoing and causes the eventual death of his father, a debt which Jimmy is forced to repay himself.

Fingers is clearly about one man's search for individual identity, with a self separate from that of his parents. Jimmy's parents are Freudian monsters, symbolic cannibals whose need has consumed their child's id whole and forced him into a state of arrested development. "I'm still short for my age," Jimmy jokes to Mr Foxx, the impresario who auditions him, an old friend of his mother's who has not seen Jimmy since he was a child. Ben, Jimmy's father, props up his waning masculinity in the company of a pneumatic raven-haired glamour model, an over-sexualized symbol of youth, who he introduces to Jimmy as his future wife. Ben equates masculinity with violence, and chides his son for not using enough force when he fails to retrieve a debt.

Ruth, Jimmy's mother, has rejected the outside world altogether. She resides in a hospital ward, where Jimmy goes to visit her. Ruth despises Jimmy because she reminds him of Ben, yet Jimmy represents both her failed marriage and its renewal. When Jimmy pecks her on the cheek, she demands a kiss on the lips.

In Jungian dream analysis the process of psychic growth by which a mature personality emerges is termed "the process of individuation". Over a prolonged period of time Jung began to see a pattern in the themes and imagery of an individual's dream life that seemed to match their psychic growth. Within the dreams certain archetypes would consistently appear as symbols of the individual's unconscious self. Jung concluded that the mature personality could only be fully realised if these symbols were consciously incorporated into the being's self.

At the very start of the film, we find Jimmy playing piano, immersed in his world of dreams. He intuitively caresses the cold, hard ivories with eyes closed, head swaying, mouthing the melody as if in thrall to some ecstatic reverie. Throughout the narrative he periodically retreats to this corner of his apartment, a secure, womb-like environment that protects him from the dangers of the outside world, sitting at the piano with his back to the wall and a window looking out onto the street to his left. According to Jung's associate, M-L. von Franz (in his essay, "The Process Of Individuation"[1]), the child will "frequently retire from outer or inner difficulties into an inner fortress" during the development of consciousness, in order to find some meaning in life that will help deal with the chaos within and outside. Keitel's own reading is that when Jimmy played piano "he was living out his fantasies... Sexual fantasies, many fantasies about love, fantasies about loneliness, fantasies about expressing his anger."[2]

Jimmy only looks at peace when he is sitting at the piano. At other times Keitel plays him as a mass of nervous tics who stutters in staccato rolls, drums his fingers absent-mindedly on the nearest surface, and plays imaginary concertos in the air. Seeing the character as somewhat eccentric, Keitel incorporated these signatures after Toback had introduced him to the work of Glenn Gould. The Canadian pianist was as famous for the eccentricities he incorporated into his performances, including audibly singing along to the score, as he was for his virtuosity.

Toback's film has no score as such. Its soundtrack is provided by Jimmy and reflects his split personality. Jimmy the aesthete, puts his all into playing Bach's *E Minor Toccata*. Jimmy, the street punk, gets off on the urgent rhythms of '50s doo-wop and '60s pop – songs by The Jamies, The Chiffons, Charlie & Inez Foxx & The Drifters – that blast out from the portable tape-recorder that almost never leaves his side when he is outside the sanctuary of his apartment. He slots tapes into the deck one after the other, playing paeans to lust and longing that outwardly project the feelings he can not fully articulate himself.

[Incidentally, Jimmy's father can not abide his taste in music. "I never understand you," he reproaches his son. "Either it's got to be a 900-year-old Kraut or 5 niggers with squeaky voices." He asks Jimmy to play a tape he has given him, Jerry Vale's crooning classic "Now Is Forever", a timeless evocation of the continuum that has passed from father to son. To Ben, the vulgarian, this cheesy cocktail lounge sound is real music, real art.]

Anyone that threatens the security that the music provides unleashes the dormant violence in Jimmy. A patron at one of the restaurants Jimmy's father dines in, objects loudly and indirectly to the music blaring out from the next table. Enraged, Jimmy gets up and begins to brawl with the man. The fight is quickly broken, whereupon Jimmy sits back down. He nurses his fury by running his fingers forcefully across an imaginary keyboard on the table, then points directly at the man, spitting out words that hint at terrific violence. "Don't you ever touch me again, you cunt," he snarls. "I'll cut your fucking lips off, you cocksucker." Jimmy arches his hands into talons and continues punching the table with his fingertips as if nothing had happened.

The primary purpose of the music in Jimmy's life is dream fulfilment. This feeling is so strong that when he first opens his eyes and shakes off his trance at the end of his practice session to find a girl staring up at him from the street, he believes she has been attracted to his performance. Grabbing the tape deck he follows her playing The Jamies' punchy "Summertime" to attract her attention. When she turns to meet the sound and sees him, he is instantly smitten.

Jimmy drives the girl (Carol) to her studio apartment on the Lower

East Side, which seems to be a repository for broken bodies, of which Jimmy is the latest. Torsos, legs, heads and arms litter her living space in the form of drawings, half-completed paintings, covered busts and sculptures impaled on metal rods. On entering, Jimmy walks past a black and white, floor to wall painting of an androgynous figure split into light and dark halves. The background on the light (left) side appears to be a rural setting of fields and forests. The dark (right) side features a cityscape crowded out by tombstones. The painting seems to represent the dualistic forces of life and death that pull at the individual.

Carol represents Jimmy's anima, his unconscious female self. Jungian psychoanalysis states that a man's anima is ruled by his mother. If the mother has had a negative influence then the anima will often express itself in irritable or depressed moods. Carol pulls away from Jimmy's initial advances towards intimacy. "Don't you understand," he pleads. "I'm going to bring you into your dreams of yourself. All you have to do is believe in me." She just looks at him coldly and says, "You're so full of shit." To Jimmy this rejection is an expression of love. Carol reminds Jimmy of his mother, who in turn rejects him because he reminds her of his father.

What Jimmy fails to understand is his need to believe in Carol. She is Jimmy's guide out of his world of dreams and into the (under)world of

Dreems, a burly, black ex-boxer turned club proprietor who is Carol's pimp and lover. This super-nigger stereotype – a powerful and dangerous symbol of unfettered male sexuality – appears as Jimmy's shadow, the unconscious self he is yet to come to terms with.

Jimmy can not gain admittance to Dreems' club without Carol, although he tries. Having being rejected by her once, he waits outside her apartment and shadows her to the club. Jimmy peers through window but his way inside is blocked by two bouncers, guardians to the underworld. He first has to be spurned by his mother, having humiliatingly flunked his audition. He goes to see Carol who tries to bar his way. But Jimmy forces his way in and locks her in an embrace. He instructs Carol to take out her diaphragm (which she does) then, still fully-clothed, mounts her in a fitful burst of pained intercourse. Von Franz states that one of the symptoms of the moods generated by the negative mother-anima is a fear of impotence. Jimmy follows Carol to the bar for a second time. In her company he is allowed entry and meets Dreems for the first time. As Jimmy's shadow, Dreems seems to understand his needs and desires and issues a challenge. He asks Jimmy to accompany him and Carol to a hotel suite, where there's a girl with a "tight, little sweet ass. A real freak. You're the motherfucker that she'd really like," he says, adding that the girl's ex-boyfriend looked just like Jimmy.

With his modish haircut, leather jacket, open shirt and neck scarf, Jimmy looks like a dandyish street punk, projecting an indeterminate sexual orientation. His appearance does not seem to stimulate the women he encounters but does attract the attention of three homosexuals at one of the restaurants he meets his father in. Midway through the narrative, Jimmy visits a urologist and undergoes an excruciating rectal examination. The doctor slips on a surgical glove, greases his finger and positions himself behind Jimmy, who is bent over the examination table. As the doctor "fingers" Jimmy's asshole, he tenses up, wriggles, squirms and moans in discomfort. Panting, Jimmy takes a tissue and wipes the lubricant out of his asshole. "What about a heroic fuck?" he asks. "You're ready to come but you're in love and the girl needs more... So do you reason with your fantasies and hold back?" "That's not a heroic fuck, that's a dumb fuck," the doc rationalises. "You're straining your prostate gland. Jimmy you got to make up your mind. Whose penis are we talking about? Yours or hers." The urologist is a symbol of Jimmy's blocked sexuality.

The simple fact is that Jimmy can't perform in public, sexually or otherwise. He humiliatingly flunks his Carnegie Hall audition. Despite re-starting the piece three times over, he continually reaches a point where he can't go any further and his fingers flail over the keyboard hitting bum notes. "I can't understand," says Jimmy, flustered and embarrassed. "I can

play this piece better than anyone alive." In his dreams.

The same thing happens when Jimmy goes to the hotel with Carol and Dreems, who offer him the chance to free himself. While Dreems caresses and kisses Christa, the girl who inhabits the hotel suite, Jimmy is expected to follow his lead with Carol, but he can't. Dreems takes Carol for himself. All Jimmy can do now is watch. He sets the tape deck down on a commode and presses play. Dreems encourages the girls to get it on together. Carol touches Christa's shoulder, but she pulls away. In a burst of unexpected violence, Dreems suddenly bangs the girls' heads together with a sickening crack. Jimmy does nothing despite being shocked and disturbed by what he is seeing. He tries to comfort Carol, but she rejects him again. The failure of this test of Jimmy's manhood symbolises the closure of his relationship to Carol, and his failure to resolve his relationship to both his anima and his shadow self.

The "head-whacking" is actually based on a real-life incident involving Jim Brown[3], for which he was arrested and later released without charge. With the complicity of Tia Farrow and Caro Francis (who play Christa), Toback decided to recreate the incident for real in the film. Apparently, the director and the three actors involved were the only people on set aware that this was going to happen. They made it "not just feel real but become real," said

Toback[4], which suggests both the lengths to which the director will go for authenticity and the autobiographical pathology of his work. The elements that make up Jimmy Fingers come from Toback himself. Born in 1944 (2 years after Jimmy), an only child to Jewish parents living in New York City, his father was vice-president of a brokerage firm, his mother was president of the League of Women Voters. According to David Thomson, Toback "adored his mother and was dazzled by a father who was himself a sexual adventurer", and is himself notorious as a sexual miscreant. He lives in an apartment "nearly blacked out" with pictures of classical composers and writers including Mahler, Strauss, Wilde and Dostoyevsky[5]. One of his childhood homes, the Majestic Apartments on Central Park West, was once inhabited by Frank Costello, "Prime Minister" in Lucky Luciano's Cosa Nostra, who was gunned down in the lobby by a mob hitman in 1957.

Toback's first stab at cinematic artistry was as screenwriter of **The Gambler**, subsequently directed by Karel Reisz and starring James Caan. (Toback is also known as an inveterate gambler, describing the experience as "essentially onanistic" and "ecstatic"[6]). After working on several script-for-hire jobs for various studios that didn't make it to the production stage, Toback wrote **Fingers** off his own back. Oddly, **Fingers** was financed by Brut Fabergé, an act David Thomson describes as "perfume trying to anoint savagery". Three days before shooting was to begin, the company tried to pull out citing lack of advance foreign sales. Toback reputedly tracked down producer George Barrie by phone in Singapore and threatened to kill him. The film began shooting with a third of the original budget forcing Toback to cut a number of scenes, including (according to Thomson) a homosexual encounter.[7]

If Toback chalked the outline for Jimmy, it was Keitel who filled in the details. The actor described the character as "a man with no identity"[8]. An interesting comment, not least because the "method" Keitel uses to play his characters requires him to create an identity for them. So, in essence, Keitel had to piece together an identity for the character only to then shatter it. He plays Jimmy as a mimic, a man who, without a sense of his own self, has inherited his modes of behaviour from his parents. A crude machismo from his father, sensitivity and fragility from his mother. Jimmy reacts to events impulsively and irrationally or not at all. To the viewer, his actions seem forced and awkward, but in the character's mind he is merely acting out what he believes he should do according to those inherited modes of behaviour.

Jimmy's mimicry is reflected in the repetition of one track on Jimmy's music box, Charlie and Inez Foxx's "Mockingbird". The mockingbird is most readily associated with the American songbird that mimics the notes of other birds.[9] His nature is also reflected in the piece of music he is practising for

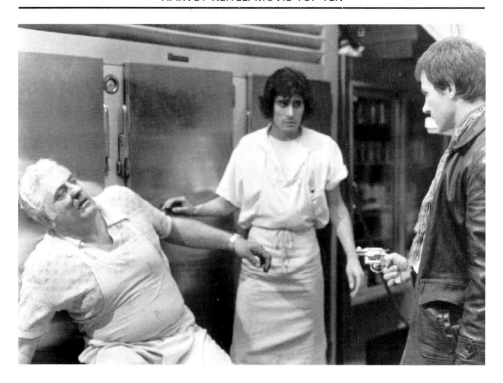

the recital – the Fugue from Bach's *E Minor Toccata*. In musical terminology, a fugue is a polyphonic composition centred around a main theme, which is "imitated" by each of the other melodic lines or voices throughout the piece.[10] It is also a psychological term for a loss of awareness of identity.[11]

The fugue is a symbol for Jimmy's journey through three interlocking narratives with thematic similarities, each of which contain a female and a male protagonist – i.e: Jimmy's mother and father, Carol and Dreems, Julie and Riccamonza. While his feelings towards his parents are barely articulated, they reveal themselves in the surrogate relationships he has with the latter two female-male pairs, which are respectively love and admiration, hate and repulsion.

Keitel also describes Jimmy as "someone who would do anything to be loved". All his actions appear motivated to please his parents. Yet he is continually rejected by his mother and put down by his father. Jimmy's piano playing is to please his mother, herself a former concert pianist, whose connections have facilitated Jimmy's Carnegie Hall audition.

Ben sees Jimmy as his enforcer, his strong arm and his right hand man. But when collecting debts for his father Jimmy makes his business personal. After pistol-whipping Luchino, the pizza parlour owner, Jimmy warns his son off with a wave of the gun saying, "You don't like what I did to your father. Well, I don't like what he did to *my* father." His downfall is

sealed when he fails to retrieve the second debt (from Riccamonza). This is pre-figured by a scene in Jimmy's apartment when Ben comes to visit him. He tells Jimmy that if he can't recover the debt, he has to get rid of Riccamonza. Jimmy looks shocked. Ben gets more worked up, baring his teeth like a wild animal. "This has nothing to do with money," he spits. "What are you going to do, put your prick up my ass," he taunts Jimmy's masculinity. "I can't, not now, dad," Jimmy says, stammering in protest like a boy given a pot to piss in.

Later that night, Jimmy is woken by the phone ringing. He picks it up. A voice says, "It's over. You understand. It's over. Don't try anything." Jimmy races to his father's apartment. The eerie emptiness is filled only by Jerry Vale's "Now Is Forever" playing on the turntable. Jimmy walks into the kitchen and finds Ben sprawled on the floor naked with half his head caved in, lying in a pool of his own blood and brain matter. Jimmy looks up showing barely an iota of grief, but his resolve is strengthened, he understands how the drama must be played out.

When Jimmy finally corners and kills Riccamonza (which, just like the hit on Frank Costello, takes place in the apparent safety of the lobby of his apartment block) it is in retaliation for the murder of his father. He is recovering the debt of his father's death, and the symbolic loss of his

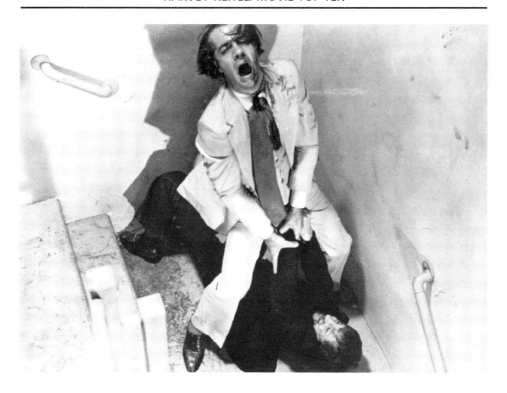

manhood, in equal measure by taking Riccamonza's balls in his hands (with his fingers) and pulling hard. He then straddles his body and shoots his eye out.

This final, act of extreme brutality sends Jimmy over the edge. The last image in the film, which plays over Bach's *Toccata* (unaccompanied for the first time), is of Jimmy sitting in the corner of his apartment. He is sitting naked, bloodied and bruised on a stool in a confined space between the piano and the outside wall of his apartment. One hand is anchored to the piano, the other presses against the window, almost as if he is acting as a link between dreams and reality but perpetually trapped in limbo between them.

As the camera tracks ever closer he turns his head, panting, to look directly out with the same remorseless stare that shows us that by giving in to his animalistic nature – using his fingers as an instrument of destruction rather than a tool of creation – Jimmy has, finally, been consumed by his madness.

If any more proof were needed of the complicity between Jimmy, his fingers and his fate, the film's title makes the link between music and criminality explicit. "Fingers" is both slang for "a pickpocket" or "informant", and musical terminology for the act of "playing a passage with fingers used in a particular way"[12]. Ultimately, it is the way in which Jimmy's fingers played the game that determined his fate.

NOTES

1. *Man & His Symbols*, conceived and edited by Carl Jung (Aldus Books, 1964) p169.

2. "The Keitel Method" by Stuart Byron, *Film Comment* (Jan-Feb 1978) p40.

3. Toback first met Brown, a former american football star turned blaxploitation staple, on an assignment for *Esquire* magazine. He lived with him for a while in L.A., wrote his biography *Jim*, and claims it was a time during which he "got to the bottom of all sexual possibilities". (See "Odds Against Success" by David Thomson, *Film Comment* [Nov-Dec 1980], p46).

4. "Notes On Acting" by James Toback, *Film Comment* (Jan-Feb 1978) p35.

5. "Odds Against Success" by David Thomson, *Film Comment* (Nov-Dec 1980) p45.

6. Ibid.

7. Ibid.

8. "The Keitel Method" by Stuart Byron, *Film Comment* (Jan-Feb 1978) p39.

9. Toback also acknowledges the idea of mimicry. "Art imitates a life which was lived in order to become a model for artistic imitation," he says in reference to the self-conscious "actor". (See "Notes On Acting" by James Toback, *Film Comment* [Jan-Feb 1978] p35).

10. "Music: An Appreciation" by Roger Kamien (McGraw-Hill, 1988).

11. Definition from *The Concise Oxford Dictionary*, 8th Edition (Clarendon Press, 1990).

12. Definition from *The Concise Oxford Dictionary*, 8th Edition (Clarendon Press, 1990).

THE RED DANUBE:
HARVEY KEITEL IN 'BAD TIMING'

"What is it men in women do require?
The lineaments of Gratified Desire
What is it women in men do require?
The lineaments of Gratified Desire"
    —William Blake, "Several Questions Answered"

It's the middle of the night, and a young American woman lies fighting for breath in the intensive care unit of a Vienna hospital. The black respirator bellows opens and closes fitfully. She has only recently been admitted, gripped in the last unconscious stages of a massive, self-induced drug overdose. Frowning surgeons have made a first incision in her windpipe. Blood flows over their white latex gloves.

Somewhere down a grey maze of corridors in the same building, two men confront each other in a bleakly formal office. A third looks on, taking notes. The first to speak is Inspector Netusil of the local police, pursuing his investigation into the reasons behind the woman's attempted suicide. "This report is from our archives," he states, crisply flicking an official-looking sheet from its clear plastic wallet. "The Germans have always been good at archives," the second man sneers back at him drily. This is Dr Alex Linden, her ex-lover, portrayed with hunched, almost glacial arrogance by Art Garfunkel. "We're in Austria," is the inspector's blank reply before he returns to his line of questioning.

It's a small moment, a pedantic correction of a minor error, but a telling one. First released in 1980, Nic Roeg's **Bad Timing** exists almost entirely in its attention to detail.

Playing with narrative conventions and slicing through the established logic of time and space, the British director organizes a series of relatively simple events into a complex pattern of sympathies, desires and hidden intentions. In strictly linear terms, the film's action is confined to the dwindling, final hours of a single night, roughly from 2AM until first light, during which an intently focused Harvey Keitel, as Inspector Netusil, examines the circumstances that led up to Milena Flaherty, played by Theresa Russell, trying to take her own life. His only witness to what has happened is psychoanalyst Alex Linden, another American, who called for an ambulance at around 1.30AM and has accompanied her to the hospital.

Describing himself only as "a friend", Dr Linden's account of what happened seems plausible on the surface, his prickly response to any further interrogation being due more to a haughty sense of his own intelligence rather than an uneasy conscience. He displays little anxiety or remorse over the woman's fate, however, and it quickly becomes clear that he has been lying not only about his relationship to Milena but also about where exactly he has been during the night, and when. According to Alex Linden, after Milena telephoned his apartment at some late hour "to say goodbye", he had driven straight over to her place and found her lapsed into unconsciousness on the bed. He can even supply a half-empty pill bottle for the doctors to identify. The rest they know.

Bad Timing's action, however, occupies a distended present in which there are no longer any fixed points. As flash-backs, triggered memories and private associations take possession of the characters, we see them react to things that were said or done in another time and space. On occasion, it is impossible to state with any precision who is speaking to whom or at what location. A sense of distance and displacement pervades the entire movie. Not only are Milena and Alex both Americans residing in a foreign country, but they also have chosen to live in the capital of one which shares a border with the former Eastern Bloc republic of Czechoslovakia. Furthermore, Milena has a husband waiting for her in Bratislava. A figure of urbane tenderness played by Denholm Elliott, Stefan Vodnik is a retired air force officer who, despite being thirty years her senior, is the only one to show Milena any real warmth or understanding.

It is to him that Milena addresses the film's opening line. Although laid out on a stretcher with an oxygen mask clamped over her mouth, her voice is clearly audible on the soundtrack murmuring, "Stefan, I'm sorry". The apology may be coming from deep within her drug coma, but it can also be taken as part of the next scene, in which Milena and Stefan are shown formally separating from each at a check-point on a bridge where the Czech river Dunaj changes its name and becomes the Austrian Danube. Such a blurring of boundaries and ambiguous sense of moment can often obscure the facts behind Keitel's investigation. Most importantly, they make it easy to forget that he has no direct contact with either Milena or Stefan throughout the entire film.

Although Keitel is first shown looking on grimly while the surgeons struggle to save Milena's life, it is Dr Alex Linden whom he asks after.

"Who is this Linden?" he demands of a subordinate. "Bit of a pain? Bad tempered?" With his long dark hair swept back into a lion's mane, his elegant white shirt, neat black suit, slim tie and loosely cut overcoat, Netusil has a flamboyant austerity about him that is completely his own.

It even shows in the long, thin cigars he chooses to smoke, taking quick sharp pulls on one between questions. Keitel endows the Austrian police inspector with the commanding presence of one who is not in the habit of wasting his time or energy. With intense singleness of purpose and the compressed moral fury of an avenging angel, he sets about discovering the truth of Milena's bid to end her life.

However, it is not his wings he is seen unfolding in the hospital office as he prepares to interrogate Dr Alex Linden, but the pages of a newspaper.

"Ah, prices today," he mutters to himself. "Tickets to Fidelio... who can afford it?" What kind of man is it that can worry about opera at so late an hour?

Perhaps Dr Linden should give serious thought to calling for a lawyer round about now. Where no detail is wasted, nothing can be thrown away either.

BAD HAIR DAYS

From its tasteful opening titles, in which the dazzling golden shards and coloured swirls of Gustav Klimt's "The Kiss" open out onto an interplay of silhouetted male and female profiles in Vienna's Osterreichische Gallerie, **Bad Timing** wears its culture with studied carelessness. A sixties movie lost at the beginning of the eighties, it offers a fragmented mosaic of references that blends polycultural liberalism with old Aquarian Age paraphernalia. Milena surrounds herself with a jumble of art nouveau *objects d'art* mixed with a glittering assortment of gimcracks, books and ornaments. A head space left over from the Prague Spring, her bedroom is littered with Klimt reproductions; images of febrile eroticism and brittle ecstasy created in Vienna at the very edge of this century and now part of the highbrow, mass-produced bric-a-brac on sale in gallery shops and museums throughout the world. The daughter of a American serviceman who had served throughout Europe, from Paris to the Czech border, she is old enough to recall the high ideals and promise of the years of Revolution.

"Poor, silly girl," is Netusil's preliminary verdict of Milena, and it's one that doesn't really change much throughout the film. He guesses she must be about 24 or 25. "A nice age," he concludes as if she were still in some sort of nursery or play-pen. He might almost be right. Milena is presented as a restless spirit, constantly experimenting both with herself and the world around her. Russell's performance would only require a few minor changes in emphasis for it to become the portrait of a dangerously deluded young woman. As it is, there is something truly unsettling about the way in which she alters her appearance from one scene to the next. Every day seems to be a bad hair day for Milena as she keeps on restyling it from tight braids and combed-over waves through to bubble cuts and elaborate perms, each new variant as playfully hideous as its predecessors. By the time Alex, whose own hairstyle conjures up some of the worst excesses of the early seventies, has finished with her, however, Milena's blond tresses will be a ragged unkempt

mess, matted with sweat.

"Is your girlfriend a bit mad?" Netusil asks with a pointed display of blandness. "Mad is an expression I never use," Dr Linden replies. Ultimately she has more to fear from him than he does from her. At first Alex Linden reads Blake aloud from her bed, listens to her records and flicks through her art books with a sense of approval. This mix of music, poetry, art and sex may be new to him, but curiosity quickly gives way to prying as the relationship turns sour. Obsessed with the notion that there are other lovers in her life, it's the snapshots of husband Stefan and her dead brother stuck casually between the pages of a Klimt catalogue that claim Alex's attention most. Apart from the photographs of Freud and Adler on the wall of his study, his own life is devoid of representational art. It is only when delivering a lecture to undergraduates on the subject of spying that he is seen manipulating projected images of people.

When challenged by a female student as to whether he might consider himself a spy, Dr Linden swiftly dodges the implication. "Well, I prefer to label myself an observer," he purrs, adding by way of explanation the enigmatic comment that, "the guilt-ridden voyeur is a political conservative." His words are followed by two juxtaposed sequences which

show Alex hanging up a suitably abstract framed print in his apartment, then Netusil at home taking down an exact copy of the same picture and hiding it away in a cupboard.

This fleeting glimpse into the inspector's domestic life reveals a diploma from Harvard University positioned neatly over a Bang & Olufsen turntable on which a Beethoven recording is playing. A young boy also appears briefly, swathed in the folds of a grown-up policeman's uniform. Keitel brings the same spare economy of movement to shooing the child gently out of his way as he displays in his dealings with Linden at the hospital. Keenly aware of his rank and duties, Netusil is very much the model of a political conservative, treating his subordinates with an abrasive formality that emphasises the difference he perceives between them.

Linden himself can also be classed as a political conservative, however. He produces psychoanalytical profiles of select individuals for American military intelligence from data supplied by army psychiatrists. The fact that he is offered no legitimate reason for doing this doesn't seem to bother him at all. He's even been loaned out to NATO. As they trade questions and answers deep into the night, Linden and Netusil emerge not only as two trained intellects used to delineating and probing the lives of others, but also fiercely self-regarding individuals. As Linden bends over the desk to put a signature

to his false statement of the facts, Netusil is struck by a sudden inspiration. He knows someone who can get him tickets to Fidelio.

"So that's what they mean by a university education," the duty officer observes sullenly, and it is impossible to tell which of the two men he is referring to.

CIGARETTES AND ALCOHOL: AN INTERLUDE

From the pack design of the Marlboros smoked by Dr Linden to the Austrian national colours, red and white form dominant motifs in **Bad Timing**'s unfolding narrative. Red, in particular, has a preternaturally strong presence throughout, occurring in the fire extinguishers and waste bins that line the hospital corridors as well as the backpacks and uniforms glimpsed in the street. Linking the highly charged flow of sexual passion with the scarlet rivulets that spring from the tracheotomy being performed upon her, the colour's strongest association is with Milena. It appears in the nail polish, jewellery and clothes she chooses, as well as in the dressing gown her husband Stefan wears after they have sex together.

Even for a film in which the main characters are constantly shown lighting their next cigarette, Milena's existence seems caught up by moments of immediacy and excess. Desire and its gratification are brought together within her as a turbulent liquid flux. She sits with Alex in his sporty red roadster talking about her two abortions and emptying one shot glass after another. When he presents her with a copy of the L??scher colour test, she wants to try it out straight away, spreading out the cards on the hood of his car while he suggests they find a "more neutral" background.

Analysis rapidly becomes a major issue of contention between Alex and Milena, their love-making shown intercut with the sterilized metal probing and bloody implements of the intensive care unit. Milena even tries to end the relationship after she discovers that Alex has been using the results of her impetuous outdoor colour test to develop a psychoanalytical profile of her for army intelligence. "I wish you'd understand me less and love me more. I wish you'd stop defining...," her farewell note reads. Their affair, however, as the unfinished sentence implies, is far from over. Alex, whose attempts to establish himself as her only lover have increasingly taken the form of physical violence against her, may soon have to give way to another; one who could prove to be Milena's last true love. Outlined in black against the white surgery wall, Inspector Netusil sternly oversees the insertion of a steel speculum as a swab is taken of the inside of her vagina.

GRATIFIED DESIRE

Netusil has his own sense of timing. There are moments when Keitel seems to be listening to a clock running deep inside his own head. As he approaches Milena's apartment in an attempt to retrace Alex's movements during the night, a very different ordering of events presents itself. It quickly becomes clear that Dr Linden took Milena's call much earlier than he has claimed. Spiteful scenarios start to unfold in the Inspector's imagination the closer he gets to the chaotic physical and emotional detritus that surrounds the American woman's bed. Alex's cold, possessive lust has already left its psychic fingerprints all over the scene of the crime. In a vile sulk over Milena's marriage to Stefan, he permits himself to be provoked into taking her violently on the stairway outside her. Intercut with his brutal rutting are close-ups of Netusil's face as if he were watching in person. Lit from below like some prying demon, his expression of satisfied fascination is almost palpable.

"Greedy bastard," Milena later throws back at Alex accusingly on the same set of apartment stairs. "You've got everything... had everything... know everything." She could also be addressing Netusil. Their closely defined sense of self is in complete opposition to the immediacy of her desires. "I'm not ambitious," she continues. "I'm not a fucking artist, or a poet or a

philosopher or a goddamn revolutionary and I don't want to have to pretend I am for anybody. I just want to be allowed to give where I can, how I can, to who I can." Alex, however, is more concerned with who she slept with the night before. He continues to seethe with frigid anger over the possibility of her sexual incontinence and takes constant issue with the untidiness of her existence.

A crazed mass of protean urges under the escalating influence of pills and alcohol, Milena transforms herself into a grotesque parody of the woman she thinks Alex must really want. Under a thickly-applied kabuki mask of white make-up and a deep crimson wig, her manic cavorting around the darkened interior of her apartment alternates between attempted suicide and a savage physical assault upon Dr Linden.

Inspector Netusil has, of course, already seen the police report concerning the disturbance. It is one of the many things that he and Alex Linden have already clashed over. The two of them exchange words reientlessly during the early stages of the investigation, correcting the meaning of each other's statements, picking away at the intentions behind each question.

Encircled by the scattered remains of Milena's apartment, Netusil's introspection becomes more apparent, Keitel slowly releasing a clenched emotional intensity as he slowly confronts Linden with the truth about Milena's suicide bid. It starts with a quiet revelation. "Why I chose this profession," Netusil falters. "A puzzle... certainly the law doesn't interest me." He closes his eyes. "When I see...," he goes on, Keitel stabbing powerful fingers at his temples. The sentence, like others in this film, remains unfinished. For someone with so little interest in the law he seems to be intimately familiar with its statutes. "The truth of the matter, Dr Linden," he says gazing distractedly at one of Milena's red shoes, "is that no one cares about Article 139B, Suicide. It has little, if any, indictable application to this case. But Article 205, Ravishment... there we have quite another apple, do we not?" The precision with which he chooses his words belies the unspeakable nature of the crime which Alex has committed. Not only did he delay his call for an ambulance by an extremely dangerous interval, but he also raped her while she lay dying.

"In a sense you take advantage of someone's love," a frowning Netusil explains, his fingers pointing upwards in fierce concentration. "You disguise your feelings of hatred." But it would be hard to dissimulate the cold fury with which Alex Linden assaults his former partner, methodically cutting away her underwear with his pocketknife. Perhaps more shocking still is the way he attempts to straighten a picture on her wall before beginning his violation of her body, or the stealth with which he removes the photographs he finds of himself in the kitchen and replaces them with snapshots of

Stephan and her brother.

Even while clutching a sheet freshly stained with Alex Linden's semen, Netusil is set upon extracting a confession, even if finally it is his own. "We are not unalike," he confides in Dr Linden. "I could understand. People who live in this sort of disorder, this moral and physical sewer. They spread it around them like a disease. Dangerous creatures... to themselves and others. They envy our strength, our capacity to fight, our will to master reality. What do they do? They try to drag us into their confusion... their chaos."

The notion of male transcendence to which both Linden and Netusil have dedicated themselves is an idealized expression of the misogyny which the two men share. Identically attired in their dark suits, white shirts and black ties, they teeter together on the edge of recognizing their true selves in each other. "Tell me what you dare not," Netusil urges, but it is too late.

Stefan breaks in on their painful grappling to tell them that Milena is expected to live. Alex shows as little joy at hearing this as he did anxiety over the possibility of her death. Netusil's response to Milena's recovery is far more difficult to read.

"Excellent! Thankful news," he states stepping away from Dr Linden,

before adding quietly: "For me, perhaps, it has arrived a moment too early."
Deprived of Linden's confession, Netusil is last seen contemplating his
bare-chested reflection in the bathroom mirror at home, hands over his head
and heart in the grip of some deep personal anguish. The taps are running,
but the water is draining away untouched. In ironic counterpoint, Roeg closes
the film with an enigmatic shot of the eternally flowing Danube. Netusil has
missed his moment of climax.

SILENT PARTNERS:
ROBERTO FAENZA'S 'COPKILLER'

Speechlessness is not a problem for Harvey Keitel. On the contrary; it's been the making of his career. Starting off as head-of-the-cast for a young Martin Scorsese, the Brooklyn-born actor crowned himself "king of blue-collar angst" via a series of films in which, typically, the lives of the working Joes he plays are thrown into chaos by a lack of self-expression. The ultimate outing in this respect is surely Abel Ferrara's **Bad Lieutenant** (1992). Here, as the corrupt cop of the title, Keitel is driven to despair by intimations of a spiritual world beyond the mire of New York that he has no vocabulary to voice. Instead, his unnamed detective mimics Christ on the cross while under the influence of heroin, and engineers a perverse act of charity towards a young nun's rapists that leads, with tragic inevitability, to his own demise.

Ten years before Ferrara's masterpiece, another New York policier did however harness the mute power of Keitel with almost as astonishing results. Variously known as **L'Assassino Dei Poliziotti, Cop Killers, Corrupt** and **Order Of Death, Copkiller** (1982) is an Italian production which consequently shares something of the Catholicism so essential to **Bad Lieutenant**. But, with Keitel's co-star being former Sex Pistols frontman John Lydon, a far more explicit debt is owed to that most daring of rock vehicles, **Performance** (1968) – a film which famously blurs Mick Jagger's stage persona with his on-screen character to enhance an atmosphere of identity in crisis.

A comparable strategy is used in **Copkiller**, as is a home-invasion plot that plays at times like an inversion of the Donald Cammell/Nicolas Roeg classic. The fact that Roeg co-directed **Performance** may even explain Keitel's presence here, as he had previously essayed a policeman opposite Art Garfunkel in another of Roeg's pop star experiments, **Bad Timing** (1980). But whatever the case, it's certainly the combination of **Performance**-style decadence with the hardboiled cynicism of the Italian cop movie that makes **Copkiller** such an unusual work – indeed, one of the most idiosyncratically reticent studies in guilt and sexual repression ever committed to celluloid.

New York is being terrorised by an assassin in a balaclava and beat cop's uniform, who uses a bread knife to slash the throats of the city's drug squad. Narcotics agents Fred O'Connor (Harvey Keitel) and Bob Corvo (Leonard Mann) appear, however, rather more concerned about the bare Central Park apartment they bought in secret four years before, presumably with dirty money.

At headquarters, O'Connor is interviewed by investigative journalist

Lenore (Nicole Garcia), a former lover and now Bob's wife. She suggests a link between the killings and police corruption, which O'Connor angrily denies by blaming the liberal press for creating an atmosphere of disorder.

Back at the flat, he meets with Bob, who is beginning to feel uneasy about their arrangement. Bob offers to sell O'Connor his half of the property. O'Connor (known at this second address as Mr Stevens) learns to his agitation that a stranger has been asking for him downstairs. That night, he is followed onto a bus by surveillance-obsessed punk Leo Smith (John Lydon).

Another murder ensues. Confronted by Smith at a stoplight, O'Connor unsuccessfully gives chase – only for the young man to turn up on the doorstep of the Stevens brownstone sometime later. He introduces himself as "Fred Mason" and claims that he is the cop killer, explaining that he has chosen the lieutenant as someone worthy of his confession. O'Connor is incredulous. But, realising that the secrecy of his double life has been compromised, he imprisons Smith in the bathroom nonetheless.

At the precinct, O'Connor can find no record of "Fred Mason". A colleague lets slip that Bob has gone to his sick mother's – code for a visit to the flat. By the time O'Connor arrives, Bob has already broken into the bathroom. To Smith's annoyance, O'Connor tells Bob about the young man's confession, and promises to sort things out.

O'Connor tries to extract a guarantee from Smith that, once free, he

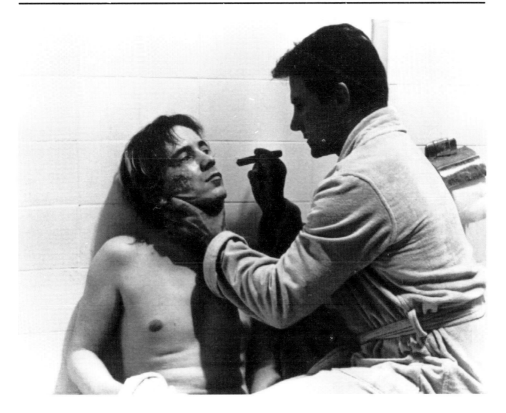

will say nothing about the apartment. The young man is uncooperative. The lieutenant begins to torture him using the kitchen gas oven, but is interrupted when Bob telephones to see if the boy has gone. An angry O'Connor arranges to buy Bob's half of the flat. When they meet for the pay-off, he pretends to have released Smith.

O'Connor re-incarcerates Smith in the bathroom, now converted to a soundproofed cell. He tells him to strip when he complains of the heat, feeds him with milk and biscuits from a dog bowl, and, after a failed attempt at conversation, contemplates burning his face with a cigar.

Bob and Lenore visit a house they are thinking of buying in the country. On the estate agent's car radio, Bob overhears a report about Smith – which, as well as the fact of his continued disappearance, reveals that he is both heir to a local fortune and a possible serial confessor.

At the apartment, Smith has heard the same report. He tells O'Connor his real name and that his grandmother is looking for him. He argues for his release by divulging that he has hidden evidence in the family home which implicates the policeman. O'Connor decides to retrieve the incriminating photographs and audiotape.

Masquerading as an investigating officer, O'Connor calls at the Smith mansion. Leo's grandmother (Sylvia Sidney) fills him in on Smith's background: the child of her son and an English showgirl, he came to America following his parents' death in a car crash; shortly after, he confessed to a nearby rape. Mrs Smith theorises that the confession was a way to atone for the guilt of inheriting his father's fortune – either that, or Leo simply enjoys punishment. As O'Connor leaves, she discloses her grandson's current fixation: a book which suggests that the police are actually agents of *disorder*, responsible for inspiring criminal acts. O'Connor intimates that Lenore is the author of the book.

On his return to the apartment, O'Connor is surprised by Bob, who pulls a gun on him in the bathroom. Bob accuses O'Connor of planning to kill Smith and, in the struggle that follows, cracks his head against the toilet bowl. O'Connor decides to dispose of his former partner by making him a victim of the cop killer.

Stealing a car, O'Connor takes Smith and the comatose Bob into Central Park. Using Bob's weapon, he holds Smith at gunpoint and orders him to cut Bob's throat. Smith denies having ever killed anyone – but, promised his freedom, does as he is told. O'Connor tries to shoot him. The pistol, however, is unloaded, and Smith flees.

The following night, O'Connor is drunk at the flat. When the doorbell rings, he prepares for his arrest, but finds Smith outside instead. The young man explains that he has returned to avoid confessing to the police that he – or, at least, some part of him – is, after all, the cop killer. O'Connor passes out. Smith examines the contents of the kitchen drawer.

In the morning, a hung-over O'Connor tells Smith that he is free to go, as Bob was already dead when his throat was slashed. Smith ignores him, and advises O'Connor to go to work so as not to arouse suspicion. Later, he quizzes O'Connor about Bob.

The next day, O'Connor is again the worse for wear. He wakes to the sound of Smith's transistor radio, and smashes it in a fit of pique. Smith, unfazed, accuses him of falling apart.

Pretending to Smith that he is checking the post at his Brooklyn flat, O'Connor calls on Lenore. She is preoccupied with the details of Bob's murder, and of the nature of his relationship with O'Connor. When she asks the lieutenant to deny that he is the cop killer, he storms out. Smith is incensed to discover where O'Connor has been, and accuses him of needing to confess. He places a new bread knife in the kitchen drawer when O'Connor's back is turned.

O'Connor visits Lenore again. She discourages him from talking about Bob. The two dine out at a Japanese restaurant, and end up spending the night together.

Back at the apartment, Smith confronts the policeman. He predicts

that O'Connor's guilt will lead him first to tell Lenore everything – and then to kill her. Expressing a desire to return home to his money, he offers to leave the apartment if O'Connor murders the woman. They begin to plan her death.

While O'Connor prepares for the murder, Smith disguises himself as his father in order to vacate the flat. The two leave together, O'Connor for Lenore's. Once there however, he simply hands over Bob's gun and reveals the existence (though not the location) of the brownstone. He promises to sell it prior to resigning from the force. Smith telephones, to hear Lenore answer. He collects a sports bag from the left luggage lockers of a subway station.

O'Connor returns to the apartment to find the phone lines cut – and, to his bemusement, Smith once more tied up in the bathroom. The doorbell rings. It's Lenore, summoned by the young man. Shocked by what she finds, she pulls Bob's gun on O'Connor. Smith accuses O'Connor of being the cop killer, and urges Lenore to call the police.

Lenore leaves in search of a phone. Smith reveals to O'Connor that, yes, he is the cop killer, and that he has chosen the lieutenant to confess for him. Impeding the arrival of the police by blocking the elevator door, he takes an NYPD uniform from his sports bag and hangs it in O'Connor's closet. He then presents the lieutenant with the new bread knife. As the police arrive, O'Connor commits suicide by slitting his throat.

Shot in New York and Rome, **Copkiller** was directed and co-written by Turin-born academic Roberto Faenza on the cusp of his fortieth year. A lecturer in Mass Communications first at Federal City College in Washington D.C. and thence at the University of Pisa, Faenza began his double life as a film-maker in 1967. **Escalation** – a scabrous, Marx-tinged satire mapping the transformation of an olive oil heir from peace-loving flower-child to murdering businessman – was followed by a trio of titles (**H2S**, 1968, **Forza Italia!**, 1977, and **Every Man For Himself**, 1980) that took the temperature of Italy in the 1970s. Then came **Copkiller**, and an eight-year break from cinema. When Faenza returned in 1990 with the Arthur Schnitzler adaptation **The Bachelor**, he had repositioned himself as the creator of serious-minded literary costume drama – making **Copkiller** a watershed project in which a youthful, quite literally punkish attitude is given its last hurrah.

Though taken from Hugh Fleetwood's novel *The Order Of Death* (Fleetwood also worked on the script in the first of several collaborations with Faenza), **Copkiller** is very much written around its pop star casting. Indeed, so predicated on Lydon's Johnny Rotten persona does the movie seem that one is tempted to explain the identity of third and final screenwriter Ennio de Concini by way of his involvement with another pop star vehicle, David Bowie's **Just A Gigolo**, four years before. The distinctive atmosphere of the film – that peculiar ebb and flow of guilt and control between O'Connor and his captive – derives in large part from an uncertainty about Smith's character enhanced immeasurably by Lydon's presence. What plagues the audience until the very last moment is how seriously to take Smith. Is he really the homicidal anarchist he claims, or merely a whining, over-indulged poseur? In other words, much the same question that hung over Lydon's head through the Sex Pistols period and beyond. And even his limitations as an actor serve to improve **Copkiller** in this respect. For, volunteering that kind of classic rock star performance which entails the occasionally clumsy importation of on-stage traits, Lydon manages to up the tension by leaving us unsure as to whether it's Smith or the man who plays him who has the penchant for amateur dramatics.

The degree to which **Copkiller** is shaped about Lydon is indicated by the way excuses are found for his English accent and personal details are smuggled in. A keen Arsenal supporter, he displays the name of his favourite team on Smith's sports bag; is, like Smith, a New York resident; manages to have his Irish parentage referred to in an explanation of Smith's mother; and smiles at the prospect of being burnt with a cigar as if recalling his own, infamous cigarette-stubbing antics. Lydon's refusal to give up drinking so as to lose weight or to cry when Keitel pulls Bob's gun on him ("you've got to keep it believable, Roberto") might also be taken as a measure of the power he wielded on set. Until **The Independent** (1998), **Copkiller** marked Lydon's only film appearance – a role in **Critters** having been turned down in 1986 – and the appeal of the movie undoubtedly lay in the manner it fell in with the singer's larger project of self-interrogation as represented by Public image Limited. Formed in the wake of the Sex Pistols' 1978 split, PiL queried the nature of the punk icon's celebrity not just in its name, but also in the bewildering fusion of styles that constituted its output. So while the legend of the Pistols was commodified in a series of fag-end stratagems masterminded by manager Malcolm McLaren, Lydon used the band to throw die-hard fans into disarray with records that drew more on reggae than three-chord thrash. In **Copkiller** also, much is made of his surprising musical tastes, with an awful stock-rock dirge (to which he rather unconvincingly dances) constituting his preferred wake-up call, and Keitel at one point – like some out-of-touch father – attempting to engage him in conversation with: "I bet you like rock music, don't you?" In which light, the end of the film might even be construed as passing ironic comment on Lydon's treatment at the hands of McLaren. Contradicting McLaren's Svengali-like claim that the Pistols were puppets and fakes, Lydon, as Smith at least, emerges as truly mad, bad and dangerous to know.

According to Lydon, relations with Keitel were rather frosty, in part because of the rigour of the latter's acting style ("Harvey [who was assigned a technical consultant] helped with his method acting. He'd be the same goddam awful git off-stage as on."). Notwithstanding, the decision to pair the two is inspired. One of the aspects of rock stardom Lydon has always studiously refused is the cultivation of any kind of sex appeal – and here, in consequence, there's an eerie lack of sensuality to his performance. Considering that most of his scenes are spent semi-nude, the net result is to amplify the already deafening silence around the true subject of the movie: namely, the fact that Keitel's character is gay.

Homosexuality is mentioned only once in **Copkiller**, and then by Lenore, who rejects the notion that there could be anything between her husband and his partner almost as soon as it comes to mind. Certainly, O'Connor and Bob seem merely to be involved in a business deal, albeit one funded by police graft. Yet in the way O'Connor notes that Bob has shaved off his beard – not to mention the way that, at the very start, he sits waiting, bath-robed, in their secret flat – there does appear to be another kind of secret activity in train. When Bob excuses the brownstone to himself as an investment, O'Connor rounds that "You bought it so that you'd have something to feel guilty about", and one is left in little doubt as to the nature of that guilt when, on selling up, Bob opts to rejuvenate his marriage by

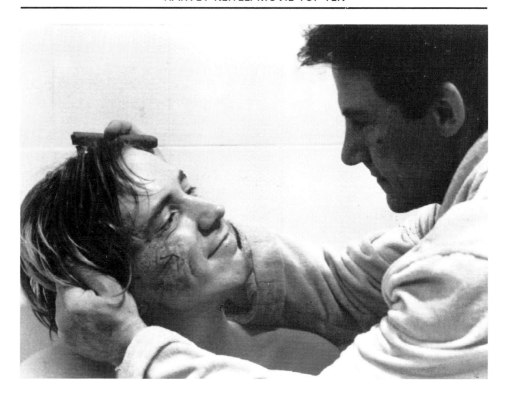

buying a clapboard house in the country.

"You know, maybe you oughta get yourself a place in the country," Bob suggests, somewhat hopefully, to O'Connor after moving out. "Me? I hate the country" is his friend's sneering reply. Preferring instead the Stevens apartment's Central Park views (habitually enjoyed while puffing on a cigar and listening to his favourite record), O'Connor certainly appears far more comfortable with his other life than is Bob. A divorcee, his last heterosexual relationship may even have been with his male lover's wife. But, as betokened by his obsessive cleanliness, tortuous theories about police corruption and oddly un-cop-like habit of always taking public transport, he too is nevertheless painfully at odds with himself. It's this which singles him out as Smith's perfect victim. As the youngster observes early on, "There's something gentle about him, something maternal, despite his tough guy act" – leading to a campaign which so besieges O'Connor's conflicted sense of machismo that, by the movie's climax, the only way out is suicide.

Enticed into making a captive of Smith so as to prevent the discovery of the apartment, the lieutenant first enters into a poisonously physical relationship with the boy in which the good cop/bad cop routine (the alternation of intimacy with the threat of violence) teeters on the brink of S/M. His identity suffers a further crisis when Smith's imprisonment precipitates Bob's murder. In fact, with the loss of Bob, O'Connor begins to take on aspects of his dead friend's persona, with Smith in turn assuming the lieutenant's former, dominant role. So now it's Smith who waits bath-robed in the flat commenting on his partner's shaving habits, while O'Connor is hen-pecked to go to work in the morning and admonished for spending the night with Lenore. (The transference makes good an association between the two characters implied early on by editor Nino Barigli's cross-cutting.) Eventually, so little is left of the lieutenant that he can no longer hide from what he actually is. As the police arrive, the need to punish himself for not being the man he has always pretended results in him becoming the cop killer – and taking his own life. In light of the twisted acknowledgement of his sexuality that the act represents, a terrible new relevance is lent Steve's *Tchaikovski's Destruction* (O'Connor's reassuringly bland record of choice) as it plays over the closing credits: "I don't believe it/Just can't control it/This is a feeling that's just changed my day".

Of course, the lieutenant's decision to identify himself with the cop killer also implies that he would rather be remembered as a murderer than gay. For O'Connor, homosexuality is quite literally "the love that dare not speak its name" – hence his absolute silence throughout the final scene. Hence also the absolute rightness of his being played by Harvey Keitel, who brings a dumb despair to these closing moments that's devastating. The effectiveness of the wordless climax is the result of careful groundwork on Keitel's part. Insinuating incoherence into even the simplest line, he consistently manages to turn O'Connor's thuggish vocabulary against itself to suggest the trauma that lurks beneath. When, in **Copkiller**'s most stylised sequence, the lieutenant drunkenly attempts to explain to Smith that "when you grow up... you have an idea... you want things to be a certain way", you know the end can't be far off – while even such throwaways as "You're not a killer. You're a psycho, a fucking psycho" are so evacuated of meaning by Keitel that they too speak of an impending collapse.

The fierce intelligence of Keitel's performance – assisted only marginally by Faenza regular Ennio Morricone's driving score – is undoubtedly what imbues **Copkiller** with the momentum so vital to its success. Minus the actor, the central conceit of placing homosexuality as a void at the heart of the film would fail disastrously; as is, it's the making of a movie where repression is the watchword even of Giuseppe Pinori's joyless, bleached-out camerawork. Given that **Copkiller** would prove to be Roberto Faenza's last picture before his transition to a more buttoned-down, middle-aged style, it's tempting to explain at least some of Keitel's intensity by way of the likeness of director to lead character: both, after all, are poised between liberation and restraint. The similarity in age between Faenza and Keitel (the actor was born in 1939), and the fact that it's Keitel rather than Lydon who gets to share a scene with old Hollywood representative Sylvia Sydney, are two pieces of evidence which might support the argument.

Be that as it may, **Copkiller** indubitably belongs to Keitel. In his hands, a fascinating exercise in punk posturing becomes excruciating human drama and the worthy successor to **Performance** it so obviously wants to be. Undoubtedly one of Keitel's finest films, **Copkiller** is also among the most uniquely compelling watches of its decade.

OLD DOG, NEW TRICKS: HARVEY KEITEL AND 'RESERVOIR DOGS'

Four Perfect Strangers.
One Perfect Crime.
Now all they have to fear is each other.

Crime Lord Joe Cabot (Lawrence Tierney) has assembled a team of five criminals, strangers to one another, to pull a diamond store heist. The crooks use color aliases, and are known to each other only as Mr. White (Harvey Keitel), Mr. Orange (Tim Roth), Mr. Blond (Michael Madsen), Mr. Pink (Steve Buscemi) and Mr. Brown (Quentin Tarantino). The heist turns into a bloodbath when the cops appear on the scene unexpectedly, and Mr. Blond starts shooting everybody at random. As best they can, the remaining criminals make their way to the original meeting place, an empty warehouse, and wait to see who, if anyone, turns up. It becomes gradually clear that they've been set up by someone on the inside, "a rat". This big question is: who?

Reservoir Dogs was the 1992 directorial debut of former L.A. video-store clerk and movie addict Quentin Tarantino, who pushed to create and promote the project from scratch, on raw talent and nerve, and on a shoestring budget. Much of Tarantino's success can be attributed to the faith and friendship of Harvey Keitel. Once Keitel signed on to do the film, impressed by the script alone, it went from an amateur production to a minimal Hollywood product, attracting $1.5 million in financing (it earned $22 million within a year). Keitel was named co-producer for his behind-the-scenes efforts to stir up investment interest and get other big name actors to audition. He says of the script, "when I read it, I was just very disturbed that here was... a new way of seeing these ancient themes of betrayal, camaraderie, trust and redemption". A longtime exponent of independent movies, Keitel often complains about the power of the big studios. In a recent interview, he comments:

"There's a stronger drive than I can ever recall [today] toward pre-packaging films and reducing the risk to zero. You have a pre-sold director and actor. The thrust has been to disregard the nature of the film itself. That cuts off the creativity of young talent, the talent that needs to explore... I'm just upset at the way things are, the unwillingness to walk the razor's edge, because at the end of it are great rewards..."[1]

Perhaps the greatest of all these rewards is **Reservoir Dogs**, a nervy, brilliant debut that proved to be one of the major turning points in American independent cinema. A cool, hip story of a heist gone horribly wrong, the film pays more attention to character development and plot than lavish sets, special effects and a Hollywood budget. And as well as being a fascinating piece of cinema in itself, **Reservoir Dogs** is an ultra-stylish homage to gangster film classics. Most obvious influences include Kubrick's **The Killing** (1956), Ringo Lam's Hong Kong actioner **City On Fire** (1987), and – most notably – the Rat Pack drama **Ocean's Eleven** (1960), which inspired the film's hallmark powerful slow-motion stroll of eight, menacing gangsters in black suits and sharp ties.

    Reservoir Dogs has been described by critics as a "postmodern neo-noir"[2], a genre typified by its overtly allusive, playful intertextual references to the classic films noir of the forties and fifties, as well as "quoting" from the neo-noirs of the sixties and seventies. Additionally, like other examples of the genre (**Romeo Is Bleeding** (1992), **Pulp Fiction** (1994), **The Usual Suspects** (1995), **Reservoir Dogs** revives the narrative devices (voiceovers and/or flashbacks) and complex structures that characterized many of the early films noir, such as **Double Indemnity** (1944) and **The Killers** (1964).

    The film first caught the attention of Miramax executive Harvey Weinstein, who recalled "it was a blow-away movie... Here is filmmaking the way we grew up with it as kids watching Bogart movies, yet it was an original voice, contemporary, not afraid to be politically incorrect, because it echoed the truth. It was like a wake-up call"[3]. Mainstream critics Siskel and Ebert gave **Reservoir Dogs** two thumbs down, abhorring its violence, and calling it "a stylish but empty crime film". The *Boston Globe* called it "the opposite of a male bonding movie; it's a male disintegration movie". The *Los Angeles Times* appreciated Tarantino's "undeniable skill", but found the film "one-dimensional", suggesting the director was "in love with operatic violence. ...The old gangster movies its creator idolizes were better at balancing things, at adding creditable emotional connection and regret to their dead-end proceedings".

Terrence Rafferty, in his review of the film in the *New Yorker*, called the film a "theatre-of-cruelty exercise", and noted that "even when nothing violent is happening on screen, we're steeling ourselves for the next bout of gore". Rafferty also believed that the film lacked "the emotional weight and sense of urgency that gave Peckinpah's films – and Scorsese's seventies films – their exploding-bullet power. Tarantino has all he can do to maintain the movie's pulse". And although Vincent Canby in the *New York Times* echoed the shocked comments of the others, he also lauded the film's "dazzling cinematic pyrotechnics", and Tarantino's awesome tyro talent.

Reservoir Dogs has been banned on video in Britain, and yet it was a huge hit there, amassing a cult following who kept it playing continuously, for more than a year, at independent cinemas like the Prince Charles in London's Soho.

Harvey Keitel, whose presence has now come to be the imprimatur of the modern crime movie, fills his role as Mr. White with a bold, edgy urgency. He paces nervously around the abandoned warehouse in his suit, runs his fingers through his hair, and sucks violently on the end of his cigarette (Mr. White smokes Chesterfields). At the sink he splashes water on his face, combs his hair, studies his ravaged, soulful face in the mirror. "I swear to God," he complains to Mr. Pink (Steve Buscemi), "I think I'm fucking jinxed." Like the rest of the gang, he's jaded, cynical and violent, but at the same time he's virtually the only character who shows any trace of empathy or compassion.

Although the film's chronology is disjointed, its structure, like that of Tarantino's follow-up **Pulp Fiction** (1996), is remarkably tight. Each scene, titled and arranged like a chapter in a book ("Mr. White", "Mr. Orange", and so on), provides a clearer view of the whole picture. It takes the whole movie to fit all the pieces together, but the nerve-damaging wait is more than rewarding. The story seems to jump back and forth in time, but in actual fact, the pre-crime and crime sequences are more interior reminiscences than flashbacks, their main purpose being not to explain, but rather to increase the film's dramatic tension. All the lead actors get their own big scenes (with the exception of Tarantino, Mr. Brown, who's shot and killed during the heist and – thankfully – never makes it back to the warehouse). Above all else, it seems – as with the subsequent **Pulp Fiction** – that **Reservoir Dogs** is a film about the art of story-telling, about the very nature of narration itself. To this effect, Tarantino employs a multiplicity of points of view that both reflects the fragmentation and schizophrenia of postmodern culture, and highlights his personal predilection for the blood-drenched pages of classic crime fiction.

Perhaps the most radical aspect of the film's chronology is that, although the whole plot centres around the heist, we never see the robbery itself, only the build-up and aftermath. This is, essentially, an action film without the action, since all the focus is on the dialogue between a small group of characters both before and after the heist. Claims Tarantino, "I ...focused on the psychodrama of the wounded, beaten guys holding an inquest on what went wrong". But although the robbery itself is skipped over, its after-effects are not, and the tense dialogue in the warehouse builds inevitably to a whirlwind of murder and betrayal, ending in a shocking blaze of glory, a violent, nihilistic Mexican stand-off.

Clearly, in terms of narrative constitution, **Reservoir Dogs** functions as both a contemporary counterpart to the classic film noir heist flick, as well as a text that very self-consciously acknowledges and investigates the history and the evolution of the noir form. Textual allusions include references to the *nouvelle vague*-influenced neo-noir films of the sixties and seventies (particularly the films of Jean-Luc Godard), and the French policiers of the fifties and sixties. There are also, of course, allusions to the classic fifties noirs of "psychotic action and suicidal impulse", as well as the Hong Kong crime cinema of the eighties and nineties. **Reservoir Dogs** is also postmodern in its successful fusion of independent filmmaking and mainstream American genre cinema. According to Richard Martin, **Reservoir Dogs** is both stylistically and thematically distinct from big-budget studio productions, especially noir pastiches like **Deceived** (1991) and **Basic Instinct** (1992): "[**Reservoir Dogs**] is connected to a number of early nineties films in the independent sector, such as **Miller's Crossing, The Grifters, After Dark My Sweet** and **Red Rock West**, that have attempted to fuse American mainstream and American art cinema filmmaking techniques in a manner intended to revive the revisionist tradition of the Hollywood renaissance filmmakers Scorsese, Penn, Altman and Coppola. Noir, as was the case with both the *nouvelle vague*'s formal and generic reinvention of western cinema and the Hollywood renaissance commodification of their techniques and experimentation, has become integral to this process.[4]"

And yet **Reservoir Dogs** is not a film about violence or action, but about this fascinating group of characters and their relationship to one

another. And to this end, Tarantino has assembled an inimitable cast. Keitel is mesmerizing as Mr. White, an experienced crook undermined by a gnawing sense of fear and anxiety; Michael Madsen is simply chilling as the sadistic and unpredictable Mr. Blond. Buscemi as Mr. Pink is a slimy, nervous weasel; Tim Roth as Mr. Orange, who spends the entire movie lying in a pool of blood, is desperate and sympathetic. Joe Cabot is played stylishly by legendary old tough guy Lawrence Tierney, who's been in and out of jail both on the screen and in real life – a real casting coup on Tarantino's part.

Unlike the run-of-the-mill gangster heist flick, **Reservoir Dogs** fleshes out even the most sadistic of crooks with a unique, multi-faceted and often sympathetic personality. There are no stereotypes here, but a set of characters with their own (albeit warped) sense of ethics. Keitel and Buscemi, for example, engage in a debate on whether or not they should take the dying Mr. Orange to hospital, thereby condemning themselves to a life in jail, and everybody seems disgusted with Madsen (Mr. Blond) for losing his head during the heist and gunning down innocent bystanders. "The most insane fucking thing I've ever seen," mutters Keitel to Buscemi, running a comb through his hair in front of the mirror. "Why the fuck would Joe hire a guy like that? ...What you're supposed to do is act like a professional. A psychopath ain't a professional."

And whilst **Reservoir Dogs** is clearly a man's movie (there's not one

single female speaking part), what makes this colourful ensemble of men so plausible and fascinating is their ultimate childish pettiness. As the story unfolds, we gradually begin to understand that these charming and charismatic outlaws, striding down the street in their matching black suits and sunglasses, are in fact no more than macho posturing, gun-happy little boys, carried away by their own juvenile love of criminals, violence and vulgarity. These are men whose sense of identity is dependent on their masculine posturings, their bravura, and their implicit capacity for violence. They're children playing at cops and robbers with real weapons, acting out their fantasies of what their favourite movie hero might do under similar circumstances – Dirty Harry, Jimmy Cagney, Lee Marvin. They're bluffers, led by some flimsy rubbed-off notion of "honour among thieves", who fall to pieces in a crisis and cry like babies, collapse into a bag of nerves, or go postal like Mr. Blond, and start gunning down strangers at random.

When the characters are assigned their colours, for example, Buscemi childishly objects to being called "Mr. Pink", and asks if his can "trade" with Keitel, Mr. White.

"You're Mr. Pink," snaps Joe, impatiently. "Just be grateful you're not Mr. Yellow".

Later, in the midst of a heated exchange of accusations, Keitel tells Buscemi, "Relax. Have a cigarette."

"I quit," he replies. Then, a moment later, "why, you got one?"

And when Keitel screams and shouts at Mr. Blond for his shooting spree during the heist, he responds like a little boy taunting another child in the school playground. "Are you going to bark all day, little doggie," he mocks, "or are you going to bite?".

What makes **Reservoir Dogs** such a powerful film, however – and what probably attracted Keitel to Tarantino's script in the first place – is the way in which it explores and analyzes the tense, dramatic dynamics of this group of terribly insecure characters trapped indefinitely in a dangerously ambiguous and claustrophobic situation. Conversations go round in circles; the fear, tension and uncertainly mount; nobody knows who they can trust, and we, the unwitting audience members, are hopelessly trapped there with them until the final credits roll. The entire plot unfolds in the same room within a couple of hours; in fact, **Reservoir Dogs** often feels more like a piece of theatre than a movie. At times, its intense, rhythmic dialogue resembles the script of a David Mamet play, or a drawing-room saga penned by Alan Ayckbourne, played out by the characters of **A Clockwork Orange** and drenched in a tide of blood. In his review of the film, Richard Corliss suggests that Tarantino's style in this respect is heavily influenced by "existential gangster films" where the crooks "talk all night about everything except what matters". Corliss describes the warehouse scenes as one "long

therapy session of bitchery and carnage... The whole production reeks of **Glengarry Glen Ross** at gunpoint"[5].

And as the gangsters indulge in their frenzied, violent arguments about who the "rat" is and what the hell they're going to do next, a deeply touching relationship begins to develop between the anguished, soulful Keitel and Tim Roth, as the mortally wounded Mr. Orange. Keitel becomes almost paternal, creating a sense of trust, and a promise to protect Orange at any cost. And this is exactly what he's challenged with, when Roth confesses that he's the rat, a cop working undercover, and his relationship with Keitel is based wholly on lies.

In effect, much of **Reservoir Dogs** can be viewed as flashbacks running suddenly through the mind of the dying Mr. Orange, a psychic death trip during which, rather than assimilating the diverse aspects of his personality in a process of integration and rebirth, his whole sense of identity unravels, culminating in his death. According to Richard Martin, "Mr. Orange may be perceived as a masculine figure marked by guilt and a masochistic desire to make amends, hence his confession to Mr. White in the film's final section and the revelation of his true, now discovered, identity"[6]. Martin also points out that there is a degree of irony in Mr. Orange's betrayal of Mr. White, in that Harvey Keitel's Charlie in the earlier **Mean Streets** is betrayed by De Niro's Johnny Boy – another example of the simultaneous movie referentiality and ironization of past films that characterizes **Reservoir Dogs**.

Ironically, the constant sense of perpetual mistrust and betrayal pervading the entire warehouse scene is the unintended result of Joe's plan that the crooks should know nothing about one another except their gang code names, so nobody can rat on anybody else. His plan, which is supposed to encourage trust, in fact has exactly the opposite effect, revealing to the crooks just how fragile and temporary their ensemble is. And since nobody knows anybody, nobody trusts anybody either, so when the heist goes wrong, any one of them – even Joe – could turn out to be the rat.

"As a writer," claims Keitel, "Quentin is in a league of his own,"[7] and indeed the dialogue of **Reservoir Dogs** crackles and blisters with violent authenticity. Tarantino has a great sense of the rhythms, role-playing and machismo of gangster street-talk, and the color-coded crooks display humour, introspection, anger, abuse and confession as they argue themselves into dead ends, going round and round in circles, analyzing what went wrong, picking at the scab of the failed heist. And the snappy, intelligent dialogue is unfailingly realistic. At one point, for example, Keitel is forced to interrupt an intense argument with Buscemi about the identity of the rat to give him some lengthy directions to the toilet:

Buscemi: For all I know, you're the rat.
Keitel [angrily]: For all I know, you're the fucking rat!
Buscemi: Alright. Now you're using your fucking head. [Pause] I mean, for all we know, *he's* the rat [gesturing to the other room].
Keitel [angrily]: Hey! That kid in there is dying from a fucking bullet that I saw him take! So don't you go calling him a rat.
Buscemi: Look. I'm right, ok? Somebody's a fucking rat. [Pause.] Where's the commode in this dungeon? I gotta take a squirt.
Keitel [resignedly]: You go down the hall, take a left, go up the stairs, and make a right.

Camerawork is also edgy and frenetic. As the tensions seem about to peak in most scenes, the camera will often start to pull back, pan away, or lead us from the scene as though it were too much to handle. This is true even for the notorious "ear chopping" scene (memorably choreographed, as Mr. Blond dances to Stealer's Wheel singing "Stuck In The Middle With You"). The illusion of violence is unforgettably brutal, but the camera refuses to let us see any of its raw, dripping details. As with the heist, we see the precursor and the bloody aftermath, but the act itself eludes us.

There's a lot of other great things about **Reservoir Dogs** – a fantastic seventies soundtrack, sharp suits, cars with fins, and one of Tarantino's

trademark gangster squabbles about the lyrics of Madonna's "Like A Virgin" and the ethics of tipping. But what draws the whole film together and gives it balance and momentum seems to be the presence of Harvey Keitel, who (for once) gets top billing. Tarantino, who refers to Keitel as the father he never had, wanted him for the part of Mr. White not only because of his stellar work with Scorsese, nor just for his recent Oscar-nominated performance as a no-nonsense gangster in **Bugsy**, but also because of his status as an icon amongst young filmmakers, surpassing the likes of De Niro and Pacino as a journeyman actor who rarely gets his name above the title. Without question, the most memorable scenes in **Reservoir Dogs** are those that involve Keitel as Mr. White; whether teasing Joe Cabot in the coffee house, comforting the dying Tim Roth, pacing frantically around the warehouse or waving his pistol around in an angry panic, this is Keitel's picture, and he knows it. Every dog has his day – and this, without question, is his.

NOTES

1. Harvey Keitel, interviewed by Ron Dicker, "Risky Business", *Salon Features* 8th December 1996.

2. See Richard Martin, *Mean Streets And Raging Bulls – The Legacy Of Film Noir In Contemporary American Cinema*, Scarecrow Press, Lanham, Md. and London, 1997: 117–118.

3. All quotations taken from Marilyn Yaquinto, *Pump 'Em Full Of Lead: A Look At Gangsters On Film*, Twayne Filmmakers Series, NY 1988: 221.

4. Martin, 20.

5. **Glengarry Glen Ross** (James Foley, 1992) is a rather stage-bound David Mamet adaptation concerning a team of real-estate salesmen, one of whom is "stealing leads" from the others.

6. Martin, 129.

7. Ibid.

"THE WAGES OF SIN":
THE TALE OF
THE 'BAD LIEUTENANT'

Skidding through the washed-out streets of New York in his cop car, the Bad Lieutenant, desperately strung out and frantic with tension, is playing the Mets-Dodgers game on his car radio. The Mets are 3-0 down in a seven-game playoff series, and trying to come back. The Bad Lieutenant has $30,000 on the Dodgers. He drives frenziedly through the city streets, snorting lines of cocaine off his wrist and knocking them back with swigs of neat whisky to level off the drug high. Darryl Strawberry strikes out; the Mets take the game. "You cocksucker!", screams the Bad Lieutenant. "You fucking miserable fucker!" In a violent fit of rage, he fires his gun into the car radio conveying the bad news, then hurriedly turns on his police siren to cover up the chaos he's causing in the streets. "You fucking shit!", he screams at the radio. "You piece of shit! You miserable slimy piece of shit! You fucking nigger fucking cocksucker! You fucking nigger piece of shit!" He skids down a side road and emits a high-pitched wail of utter anguish...

"For we wrestle not against flesh and blood, but against... spiritual wickedness in high places"
                                                                    —Paul iv.12

In Abel Ferrara's coruscating vision of the City of Dreadful Night, Harvey Keitel gives a relentlessly powerful performance as the nameless Bad Lieutenant – an authority figure of pathological corruption wreaking havoc on the hellish streets of New York. Keitel is a psychopathic, alcoholic cop at the far end of a fatal cocaine habit – a john, a junkie, a gambler, a killer, and a thief. Between lifting evidence from the scenes of violent crimes, he stumbles from smackhouse to brothel to bar, from hooker to hooker, from Harlem to Hell's Kitchen.

In one scene, he's scoring smack from a black dealer on a dark tenement stairwell when he hears voices on the lower landing. "Get back! Police activity!", he shouts down the stairwell, flashing his badge, then gets back to scoring his deal. Later the same night, arriving at a grocery-store hold-up, he demands a cold Bud and a packet of cigarettes from the terrified proprietor before shooting his gun at random into the shelves of canned goods, and stumbling around the store, waving his weapon, helping himself to groceries. He snorts coke off a picture of his child at communion. He visits a blonde prostitute just for the sensation of someone touching him. He presents her with a bottle of champagne, finishes it off, and moves on to neat whisky which he swigs from the bottle while dancing, shirtless, with a pair of hookers. "That's my bad lieutenant," says the blonde to her friend, proudly.

Keitel, his face perpetually covered in a thin film of sweat, his hair constantly tousled, his ongoing anguish betrayed by a series of muscular tics, leads the Bad Lieutenant towards a traumatic existential crisis in his life and career – a trauma that turns out to be fatal. Keitel's performance is creative, resourceful, convincing, and free from any artifice or mannerisms. Never upstaged, he holds nothing back. Anyone else sharing his screen space becomes virtually invisible.

"I am come to destroy the law"
—Matthew ii, 17

Bad Lieutenant presents us with a disabling vision of a world gone to seed, a city in which all moral and ethical systems have failed, in which the family unit has collapsed, a city of endless hypocrisy, of sins and falsities, of social and economic chaos. Like Travis Bickle in **Taxi Driver**, Keitel's Bad Lieutenant is wracked by an endless feeling of loneliness, of the absence of belonging, an irreversible estrangement and anomie. Unlike the Taxi Driver, however, the Bad Lieutenant makes no radical gestures of heroism or idealism, but instead abandons himself to the chaos of the city streets, abuses his position of authority, steals, snorts cocaine, gambles, takes bribes, ignores his duties, demands blackmail.

At times there is humour in the Bad Lieutenant's recklessness, even though this is so clearly a portrait of a man in great distress, at the edge of the abyss, traumatized by spiritual guilt. There is humour in the torment because humour is so significant a part of what it means to be a human being. At one point, he arrives at a crime scene in which two girls have been shot, Son-of-Sam-style, in the front seats of their car. "I don't know if they're still wearing the rounds in their heads or what," remarks one cop, desultorily. The Bad Lieutenant takes a cursory look at the crime scene and doesn't deign even to reply, changing the subject to the baseball game, inviting everyone to share their thoughts on the Dodgers' prospects – even some of the crime scene witnesses.

When called to the scene of a black man with his throat cut, the Bad Lieutenant simply ransacks the murdered man's car, attempting to lift a bag of cocaine. In another scene, he stops two under-aged girls for a broken tail-light, and discovers they're driving their father's car without a license. He peers in the driver's window, negotiating a sleazy exchange of sexual favours in return for his silence, masturbating surreptitiously outside the car door as he sexually intimidates the women. "You being bad girls, huh?", he asks them roughly. "Got any drugs in the car? Any drugs? Where were you tonight, huh? ...C'mon, I know what it's like to get high a little bit, to get stoned a little bit. You got any drugs on you? Any grass? ...Tell you what, you do something for me and I'll do something for you, whaddya say about that? You do something for me, and your father won't know you took his car without a license, whaddya say about that?"

"He that humbleth himself shall be exalted"
                                            —Luke xiv, ii

There is nothing in this shattered world that is pleasant or uplifting – no kind gestures, no thoughtful words. In this universe of broken laws, hate-filled hypocrisy, murder and atrocity, the bedeviled Lieutenant is cast adrift with no moral or ethical anchors by which to ground his identity, his ego, his sense of selfhood. His relationships with police colleagues are aggressive and laconic; his family is vague and nebulous; his friends – many of them fellow cops – are pimps, hookers and smack dealers. His character is symptomatic of the world he lives in. We never learn how he came to be the way he is – it doesn't matter. This is a morality play, a Canterbury Tale for the Millennium, the story of a man without a name, the Bad Lieutenant, Everyman in the depths of moral corruption and spiritual trauma. It is not a story with much of plot; there is no case to solve, no crimes to stop. This is not a mystery, a cop movie or a love story but a close study of character, of a man besieged by the demons of need and dread, addicted to fast-failing temporary remedies, gnawing bitterly at the end of his tether. Equally uncomfortable in body and soul, each depraved act committed by the Bad Lieutenant is simply another attempt to lose himself, to seek love, to escape from the terrifying predicament of being who he is by striving to avoid the constraints of the ego, the manacles of consciousness.
      And yet just as he commits violence on others, he also commits violence on himself – not only the physical violence of drug and alcohol abuse, but emotional and spiritual violence, which are worse. His rage is directed at himself, and at a God he believes has neglected him, and to whom he draws himself closer through wilful, self-flagellating defiance.
      In this world without rules, without laws, the Bad Lieutenant finds one single touchstone of significance: the game of baseball, with its unambiguous regulations and prohibitions, its final and unassailable set of governing practices. For the tormented Lieutenant, baseball is a world of laws and rules, a last haven of truth and value in a city gone to seed, a cesspool of sin, self-loathing and defilement. The narrative itself attains a semblance of structure only by virtue of the seven game playoff series between the Mets

and the Dodgers, thematically paralleled by the lieutenant's systematic infraction of the seven deadly sins.

Waking up fully clothed on his sofa at home, he ignores the baby girl who clamours for his attention and turns on the television instead, to catch up on the game. The Mets are winning. The next day, grimacing in disgust, he turns off the police radio messages in his cop car to discuss the game with his partner. He drives to a bar with a group of other cops to put money on the game, which they watch on a small, dark TV screen. "I'll tell you one thing now, I'll tell you one thing now," comes the voice of the sports commentator. "The longer this series goes, the longer this series goes, the Mets are gonna get tight." One of the cops, played by Victor Argo, claims the series is being drawn out for commercial endorsements. "Wanna make a smart move?" he asks. "Leave it on the Mets." The Bad Lieutenant, nearing the limits of self-inflicted human pain, all his money on the Dodgers, pulls out a comb and runs it through his tousled hair anxiously. He loses another $30,000 on the next game.

"Be not overcome of evil"
—Romans xii. 21

And yet despite all his cynical braggadocio, the Bad Lieutenant clings desperately to his faith that the favourites must win. Refusing to cut his losses, he staggers to a darkly lit bar to watch the next game. The Mets are still 3-0 down in a best of seven series and struggling against elimination by the Dodgers. Red-eyed and frantic, he makes his way to a strip club and stumbles through the strobe-lit dancers looking to score some cocaine. After standing a deal outside the club, he makes his way to another bar to meet a friend of his Mafia bookmaker. The Bad Lieutenant is drunk, tense and stoned. The more anguished he gets, the more extreme and suicidal his faith in the Dodgers. He's blindly convinced the favourites have to win the series. "It never could have gone any other way," he insists. "Never could have gone any other way."

The mobster middleman refuses to take his bet and leaves him with the bookmaker's number. Sitting alone in the darkened bar, the Bad Lieutenant begins laughing uproariously to himself, unable to stop. He spends to following day in an agonized haze of blind, drunken faith in the Dodgers. The closer the game becomes, the more extreme and unthinking his faith. He calls the bookmaker to place his final bet from the cop car, eyes wild and bloodshot, paranoid, waving his gun in his left hand. Red-faced and disheveled, he screams down the telephone. "Put in my bet!", he screams, furiously. "There's nothing to think about! Either you put in my bet, or you get nothing! I ain't no fucking asshole, I'm a cop!"

Unlike Charlie, the gangster played by Keitel in **Mean Streets**, no emotional loyalties or family obligations bind the Bad Lieutenant. Nor, however, is he entirely evil, like the character of Sport, the half-breed pimp played by Keitel in **Taxi Driver**. Despite his bitter and cynical disregard of the violent crimes taking place around him on the street every day, the Bad Lieutenant is shocked into a sudden desire for justice by the particularly brutal rape of a nun (played by Frankie Thorn) on the altar of a local Catholic church in Spanish Harlem. At first, when the police want to put up a $50,000 reward for information leading to the arrest of the rapists, the Bad Lieutenant is baffled.

"The church is a racket," he says to his police colleagues in the bar.

"So what?" one cop replies. "Are you a Catholic?"

"I'm a Catholic," says Keitel, defensively.

"Then why don't you have a little bit of fucking respect?" complains the cop.

And gradually, the more dissolute and disheveled he becomes, the more obsessed the Bad Lieutenant grows with the raped nun. He's drawn to her pain and her piety. Her rape becomes the pivotal incident in his ongoing emotional and spiritual crisis, the dividing line between his past and his future. He hides in the hospital to overhear the crime report ("here are the soiled undergarments and the nun's habit. They're to be taken by you for evidence... There was trauma to the vagina mucosa with multiple lacerations in which the hymen was broken... it was stated that the object was a crucifix"). He sleeps on the floor of the desecrated church, whisky bottle in hand, and wakes up to overhear the nun's confession, in which she describes the crime to her priest. "Those boys," she says in a gentle voice, "those sad, raging boys, they come to see me as the needy do. And like many of the needy, they were rude. Like all of the needy, they took. Like all the needy, they needed. Father, I know them. They learn in our school, and they play in our schoolyard, and they are good boys... never again will I encounter two boys whose prayer was more legible, more anguished..."

"Father, forgive them, for they know not what they do"
—Luke xxiii, 34

The rape of the nun is an uncompromising display of violence beyond even the comprehension of the ungovernable Lieutenant. At last, he's come face to face with an act so atrocious that retribution seems not only unnecessary, but an urgent imperative. In a confused attempt both to come to terms with the crime and to seek relief from the tension of the baseball series, he wanders through the dark, peaceful interior of the church, his shirt open, swigging from a bottle of whisky and swaying from side to side. The church

still bears evidence of the recent desecration – bloodstained crucifixes, the word "fuck" scrawled across a painting of the Last Supper, yellow police crime scene tape, a smashed icon of the Virgin Mary shattered on the floor, beside which the Bad Lieutenant lies down and quickly passes out. When he wakes, his face and hair a dusty mess, he immediately takes a drink from his whisky bottle and makes his way home to snort a line of coke. Later that night, he makes his way into the quiet of a child's bedroom where he picks up and rocks a small baby, crying and muttering to himself gently.

The next morning is the day before that of the decisive ballgame. Keitel, a lurid glut of neuroses, a strung-out mess of tics and twitches, makes his way to the home of a fellow cop, a Hispanic, and collapses beside his friend's elderly mother on a sofa covered in an embroidered cloth depicting a garish tableau of Christ. The room is filled with glowing votive candles. A quiz show is playing on television. Keitel, his eyes desperate with longing and need, leans over to the old lady and clutches on to her arm. She bends over his pained face, as if waiting to hear his confession. Virtually comatose, he can manage only a hoarse whisper.

"Dodgers gonna win tomorrow," he rasps.

"Yes, I know," says the old lady, nodding.

The other cop returns with $30,000 in an engraved rosary box for him to put on the Dodgers. The old lady adds a rosary and crucifix to the cash in the box, and the Bad Lieutenant kisses her, takes the money, and staggers drunkenly down the dark stairwell of the sordid tenement building, gun in

hand. Flickering shadows play on the walls of the staircase. The sound of dripping water merges with the distant voices of children, shouting in Spanish. Out on the street, the blazing heat and loud throb of car stereos extend the impression of hell. But the Bad Lieutenant can look right into the bowels of hell and bluff it, without flinching. "I can't die... I'm blessed... I'm a fucking Catholic," he boasts, inviting the mobster to come after him, knowing he can face any danger down. But in his black heart, the Bad Lieutenant knows that he's reached the end, that all his actions now are recklessly self-destructive. His quest for love has led only to death.

"...there shall be weeping and gnashing of teeth..."
—Matthew viii, 12

Unable to bear the tension as he waits for the start of the game on which he's staked $60,000, the haunted lieutenant makes his way to the home of a nameless prostitute (played by Zoe Tamerlis, co-writer of the screenplay with Ferrara) who injects him with heroin. "Vampires are lucky," she tells him as she injects a speedball into his arm. "They get to eat on other people. We've got to eat away on ourselves. We gotta eat our legs so we get the energy to walk; we gotta come so we can go, we gotta suck ourselves off, we gotta eat away at our souls until there's nothing left but appetite. We give and give and give crazy – a gift that makes sense ain't worth it. Jesus gave seventy times seven. No-one will ever understand why, why he did it..."

The following morning, tearing frantically around the city listening to the game on his police radio, Keitel is unable to bear the tension any longer and takes refuge in the church once again. In a subtle blending of two rule-based rituals, the non-diegetic soundtrack of the baseball game backs up images of the raped nun involved in her prayers. Finally able to ignore her no longer, the Bad Lieutenant staggers up the aisle of the church and kneels down beside her. The following conversation takes place:

Bad Lieutenant: Listen, to me sister, listen to me good. The other cops would just put these guys through the system. They're juveniles, they'll walk. Get it? But I'll beat the system, and do justice. Real justice. For you.
Nun: I have already forgiven them.
Bad Lieutenant: C'mon lady. These guys put out cigarette butts on your... Get with the program. How could you...? How could you forgive these motherf... these guys? How could you...? Deep down inside, don't you want them to pay for what they did to you? Don't you want this crime revenged?
Nun: I have forgiven them.
Bad Lieutenant: But... do you have the right? You're not the only woman in the world. You're not even the only nun. Your forgiveness will leave blood in its wake. What if these guys do this to other nuns? Other virgins? Old women who die from the shock? Do you have the right to let these boys go free? Can you bear the burden, sister?
Nun: (emphatically, turning to him) Talk to Jesus. Pray. You do believe in God, don't you? That Jesus Christ died for his sins?

"A candle of understanding"
                                        —2. Esdras xiv. 25

As the nun leaves him at the altar, the Bad Lieutenant is totally traumatized by her forgiveness. Vengeance is all he knows. The idea of forgiveness is terrifying to him, because if such a monstrous crime as these two young crackheads have committed can be forgiven, the implication is clear: redemption may still be possible, even for him, a creature with only vestigial traces of his humanity intact. There is a slender ray of hope even in the suffocating darkness, and that is almost too much for him to bear. The desperate Lieutenant falls to his hands and knees and begins to groan and bay at the altar, reduced to the howlings and yelpings of a beast in pain, crawling down the church aisle on all fours. He has descended into madness. A vision of Christ, hallucinated, appears in the aisle before him, and instead of bowing in reverence, Keitel hurls a rosary at him, casting insults and blasphemies, howling in anguish, wailing and clutching at his head in an

agony of repentance and regret. "You fuck! You fuck!" he howls at the vision. "Where were you? Where the fuck were you? I'm sorry... I'm sorry... I did so many bad things. I'm sorry. I tried to do... I tried to do the right thing but I'm weak, I'm too fucking weak. Help me, I need you to help me, forgive me, forgive me please." Beside himself with guilt, self-loathing, spiritual agony and the desperate hope of salvation, he begins kissing the bloodstained feet of the hallucinated vision of Christ. Suddenly, the vision disappears and is replaced by an elderly black lady returning a holy cup, which she found in her husband's shop. It's a cup that was stolen during the rape. The Bad Lieutenant has been granted knowledge of the rapists' identities.

"...the voice of him that crieth in the wilderness..."
—Isaiah xi. 3

Keitel, his clothing in disarray, his eyes wild, follows the old lady back to a drug den where two Hispanic boys are sitting watching the baseball game on television. He handcuffs them and points his pistol at their heads, but, unable to tear himself away from the game, joins them on the sofa to watch the end of it. His quest for retribution momentarily takes second place to his obsession with the baseball tournament, as he gets the rapists to light his cigarettes, at one point even sharing their crack. The Mets win the championship. The Bad Lieutenant is lost. Unable to pay back the $120,000 he now owes, he knows his bookkeeper will kill him on sight. He rounds up the handcuffed boys, marches them out of the cellar, forces them into the back of his car, and starts driving madly, right on the very edge of meltdown.

"You raped a holy thing!" he screams at them, the game forgotten. "You destroyed that young girl. And she forgives you. You hear that? She forgives you. Watch this, you motherfucker–" he smacks them with the butt of his gun – "you cocksucker, fucking scumbags, you fucking scumbags, I ought to blow your fucking face apart... and she forgives you. How could she forgive you slimy little bastards? How could she forgive a thing like that?" Almost out of his senses, a desperate mess of twitches or tics, he marches them at gunpoint to the Port Authority Bus Terminal and puts them on a bus, but not before handing them the box containing $30,000 in cash, the rosary and the crucifix. The bus doors close. He has forgiven them. The vision of Christ in the church has transformed his world, enabling him to make this enormous gesture of forgiveness, of which he would have been incapable an hour before. And by extending forgiveness to others, he qualifies for forgiveness himself.

And then, in public, in the bus terminal, the Bad Lieutenant resumes his agonized baying and howling, crying aloud as he walks back to his car, which is parked under a huge sign which reads "It All Happens Here". The elegiac romantic closing music begins: "Pledging my Love" by Johnny Ace. "Forever my darling, my love will be true. Always and forever, I'll love only you". As the Bad Lieutenant gets into his car, he's suddenly hit in a drive-by shooting – presumably the hitman he was anticipating. The bus with the two boys on it, pulling out of the terminal, drives past. An idle crowd begins to gather, slowly, around the crime scene.

"PERFORMATIVE HYSTERIA": GESTURES OF MALE MASOCHISM IN 'DANGEROUS GAME'

"The dramatist thereby creates a neurotic space where the spectator may live out their conflicts and even gain masochistic satisfaction in identifying with the hero's defeat."[1]

INTRODUCTION

In the article "Psychoanalysis And The Theatrical", Elizabeth Wright tries to account for a certain type of dramatic, theatrical performance which forces its characters to explore extreme states of emotional and psychological trauma. Rather than presuming that these types of fiction are totally the result of scripted dramatic requirements, Wright argues that they also draw on the unresolved tensions of childhood sexuality.

These infantile drives (with their contradictory traces of Oedipal desire and hostility), have traditionally been traced through the psychoanalytical study of mental aberrations such as hysteria. Here, the sufferer's adolescent or adult body bears the signs of these irresolved tensions through a series of uncontrollable spasms, shudders and uncoordinated physical gestures. By arguing that "theatricality becomes the operative factor both in consulting room and on the stage"[2] Wright argues that an excessive acting style can equally be read as "symptoms" of the libidinal.

This effect is even more marked in those types of performance where the split between the actor and their fictional role has been blurred. As in the case of extreme psychological disorders, the ambiguity around the fictional and the (presumed) persona implies that the very core of unified identity has been fragmented. Wright's conclusions about the theatricality of performance indicates that such productions are actually exploring an "other scene".[3] This occurs outside of the domain of scripted action, and in referencing the child's forced negation of a parental love object, ultimately draws on prior states of suffering and humiliation.

In linking the hysterical and the performative, Wright's analysis becomes a useful tool for interpreting the recent career of Harvey Keitel. Over the last ten years, the actor's screen fortunes have been regenerated through being cast in a series of roles in controversial films such as **Reservoir Dogs** (1992) and **Pulp Fiction** (1994). Although initially associated with the work of Quentin Tarantino, Keitel's revised screen image has also centrally been associated with the two controversial films he made with director Abel

Ferrara.

Many of these recent roles reference a type of "toughness" which has become the actor's trademark since his casting as the aspiring underworld charge hand Charlie Cappa in Martin Scorsese's **Mean Streets** (1973). However, they also over-emphasise the elements of self-doubt, familial and religious guilt which underscored this character. Thus, while Keitel's performance as a sadistic and morally bankrupt cop in Ferrara's **Bad Lieutenant** (1992) *appears* to indicate a security around the protagonist's sexuality and identity, these elements are countered and undercut by the degree of self-doubt and near-masochistic introspection which Keitel brings to such roles.

What interests me in this revitalisation of the actor's career is that roles such as **Bad Lieutenant** are also premised on an engaging, yet irrational and frequently hysterical form of acting and display. In this respect, Keitel's "style" of performance mirrors that of Dennis Hopper, whose career also underwent a renaissance with the release of David Lynch's **Blue Velvet** (1986). Both actors rely on excessive physical movements and manic gestures whose impact leaves an audience questioning if they have witnessed an excessive "fictional" performance or a *genuine* display of mental aberration.

In their creation of "these spectacles of madness" Hopper and Keitel clearly reference the symptoms of hysteria that Wright argues underscore performance as psychological disturbance. Equally, the fragmentation of identity that these roles provide is furnished by the fact that they clearly draw on an established set of extra-cinematic factors relating to the real life, unconventional (and well publicised) backgrounds of both actors. In the case of Hopper, his past as a hell raiser and drug-fuelled movie maverick are frequently used as a factual index for roles such as Frank Booth in Lynch's film.

As Marshall Fine has noted in *The Art Of Darkness*, Keitel is also an actor whose roles reflect a particular brand of personal investment. Indeed, as the actor has himself commented, "I am usually attracted to a role because it mirrors something I am grappling with in my own life".[4] However, even more than Hopper, the focus of Keitel's factual investments are extremely personal, and involve him having to work through of a large degree of suffering and humiliation.

By considering his role in the Abel Ferrara film **Dangerous Game** (aka **Snake Eyes**, 1993), I wish to consider Keitel's acting style as symptomatic of a type of "performative hysteria", akin to the patient whose body inadvertently displays the echoes of unrepressed Oedipal trauma.[5] The reason for my choice of this film as a case study is twofold. Firstly, Ferrara's movie is marked by a self-reflexive film-within-a film mechanism based on and around the movie set of director Eddie Israel (Keitel). The resultant blurring

of the boundaries between the fictional and the real life persona of the star provides an example of the dissolution of distinct identity which Wright outlines. Secondly, by focusing on Israel's gestures of near-hysterical suffering and torment, the film complicates established readings of the star's roles as primarily vehicles for self-assured sadism.

LIGHTS, CAMERA AND... AGGRESSION!: THE SELF-REFLEXIVE PERFORMANCE OF MASOCHISM IN "DANGEROUS GAME"

The plot of **Dangerous Game** centres on the production of the latest film by director Eddie Israel. Entitled *The Mother Of Mirrors*, it explores the conflict between spiritual redemption and physical transgression through the metaphor of a couple's disintegrating marriage. The choices between the spiritual and the sexual that the protagonists are forced to make are neatly defined by the differing traits of the two central characters that Israel's film depicts.

In the figure of Claire (Madonna), Israel depicts a character divorcing herself from a former lifestyle of orgiastic behaviour and hedonistic drug abuse which prevented herself and her husband Russell from examining the fault lines in their relationship. By seeking redemption via religion, Claire finds her actions constantly challenged by Russell (James Russo), who finally executes her after physical and mental torment have failed to dissuade her from this spiritual quest.

From the brief description of the plot already given, it becomes clear that *Mother Of Mirrors* extends beyond its boundaries as "fictional" production to make a series of wider references about established interests and preoccupations of the personnel involved in the production of **Dangerous Game**.

Centrally, these self-referential strategies revolve around Keitel's persona while clearly linking these concerns to other work in the actor's repertoire. For instance, Israel's film with its division of transcendence and physical excess replicates a series of choices that Keitel has had to make both in his own life and through his fictional characterisations. As he commented to Marshall Fine:

"Man must descend into the darkness to find the light. If there is any frontier, it is downward, not upward. What is fact or fiction? Sometimes art imitates life; sometimes it leads life. Hopefully we transcend the place we're standing in."[6]

Importantly, his comments relate to his experiences of working with Abel Ferrara on **Bad Lieutenant**, and the concerns which dominate **Dangerous Game** can very much be seen as an extension of those foregrounded in that earlier film. However, what is also central to Keitel's two performances for the director, is that their production coincides with an intense period of emotional turmoil occurring in his actual life. This non-fictional drama began in 1991 when he discovered that his wife was engaged in an extra-marital affair. The fact that Keitel's partner at the time was actress Lorraine Bracco and her co-adulterer actor Edward James Olmos, instantly adds a level of "unreality" to the proceedings. (This is confirmed by the fact that this relationship emerged from fictional roots: an encounter on the set of the 1990 film **A Talent For The Game**). In the emotional turmoil that followed this revelation, the couple's break-up gained further "mythical" value via the press reporting status of "celebrity couple in crisis"; which has become a regular feature in the trade magazines that circulate around Hollywood. According to Marshall Fine, the blurring of fact and fiction reached its conclusion in the 1993 divorce court settlement which saw Keitel lose his home and unrestricted access to his daughter.

Central to Bracco and Olmos' defence was the allegation that the violence and sadism that had been central to many of his famed performances had actually spilt over and affected his everyday behaviour. As Bracco argued, "I terminated my relationship with (Harvey Keitel) because I could no longer tolerate his abuse of me. Harvey Keitel is addicted to abuse".[7]

It is interesting that the actor responded to a situation already heavily coded as fictional, by apparently exporting his pain and humiliation into roles that reflected his feelings of suffering during the period. Of **Reservoir Dogs**, he is stated as saying that his initial interest in Tarantino's script related to its themes of honour and betrayal so pertinent to his feelings at the time. In the case of Ferrara's **Bad Lieutenant**, the actor was attracted to the dialogue it opened up between redemption and (self) hatred. These themes, again, clearly relate to the wider events circulating in his life at the time. According to Marshall Fine, the role allowed the actor to express not only his sadistic feelings towards the couple, but also gave expression to a more masochistic expression of loss and isolation:

"...dealing with all the most dangerous and destructive emotions within, was and is a kind of therapy, a way to express those feelings in a constructive manner that does no damage to anyone else: not a catharsis, exactly, but an understanding, a coming-to-terms. It was frightening to Keitel, who harboured deeply anti-social urges inspired by the dissolution of his household and the loss of Bracco. Here was a chance to actually go crazy, in a way that wouldn't land him in jail."[8]

It seems more than mere coincidence that Fine's description of Keitel's feelings at the time could easily fit the classical psychoanalytic description of the Oedipal child enraged to discover his affection for a desired parent has been rejected. Indeed, while Keitel's comments clearly fit a very adult form of "loss" he was undergoing, they also relate to the fact that this marital break-up coincided with the death of his mother. This seems pertinent as *The Mother Of Mirrors* is continually coded with references relating to the infant's loss of the mother's body as a source of comfort. In one scene Israel even defines Russell's alienation from Claire as a "kind of death", like "a child who has lost his mother's tit".

Equally, although the trauma experienced by Keitel was effectively worked through in the roles he undertook at the time, it was by no means the original source of discomfort that had inspired him to become an actor. According to Marshall Fine, the true basis to the profession that Keitel was destined to assume came from a verbal stammer which afflicted his childhood. This forced him to adopt a variety of guises and roles in order to detract from the insecurity he felt about the impediment. The stutter (which lasted well into Keitel's teens) is defined by the actor as something which "disturbed" the formation of his identity. It is a disorder which Marshall Fine attributes to a mental conflict related to the actor's fear of being governed by "rigid" parents as a youngster.

As Keitel himself comments, "Stammering is an attempt to stop the

assertion of the self"; its appearance was accompanied by physical symptoms of discomfort, such as the feeling of choking. This disorder as the basis of the actor's identity draws close parallels with Wright's consideration of performance as an extension of maladies such as hysteria. The fact that the stammer emerged between the ages of five and six adds to a potential Oedipal reading of his performances in recent productions.

These links between the hysterical, the libidinal and the theatrical are further facilitated in **Dangerous Game**, by the fact that Ferrara closely modelled Israel's character around elements of Keitel's past. Even the resonances of the character's surname carry over from the depicted fiction by virtue of the star's well documented quest for spirituality through a rediscovery of his Jewish roots. The fact that he was a Marine based in the Middle East during 1957 when he began this search, underscores the use of "Israel" in his title. Indeed, *The Mother Of Mirrors* even parodies these earlier life experiences by screening video tape material of *Israel* commenting that *his* former life as a Marine confused a search of spirituality with acts of physical brutality.[9]

Beyond the overlap between the personalities of Keitel/Israel, *The Mother Of Mirrors* complicates coherent constructions of the self by having its conflict between physical abuse and spirituality bleed over into the lives of the protagonists involved. Most obviously, if the quest has dogged Keitel's own existence, then it is replicated as afflicting Israel's decline prior to his death in the final scene of **Dangerous Game**. However, the film complicates this struggle further by highlighting the transgressive effect the production has on the personalities of its principal actors.

Most noticeably, Frank Burns (whom Israel casts as Russell against the wishes of production executives) begins to replicate his character's scripted verbal assaults against Claire as a means of denigrating the acting ability of Sarah, who is performing the role. Equally, the brutal rape scene which forms the ultimate assault on his wife has to be halted by production hands after it becomes clear that Burns has actually penetrated Sarah against her wishes, rather than sticking to the scripted, simulated intercourse that the scene requires.

Although Israel is initially critical of Burns' obsession with using the script as a mechanism to torture his co-star, it is pertinent that he preps him off-screen for the more controversial scenes by denigrating Sarah/Claire with a barrage of negative and highly sexual jibes against her character.[10] This can be seen as further evidence of an erosion in Israel's ability to limit his anti-social urges to the production he is engaged in. Indeed, the controversial scene of sexual assault that he "directs" Burns to undertake against Sarah, he later replicates against his own wife when he cajoles her into an act of intercourse in the back of a car. (The fact that Israel's wife is referred as "Maddie" further blurs the film's fictional boundaries by linking her to Madonna, who is cast as Sarah/Claire).

The self-reflexive film within a film mechanisms employed by **Dangerous Game** were roundly dismissed by critics such as Leah Rozen who argued "This is a stupefyingly bad movie. And boring. And pretentious..."[11] However, Ferrara's film does confirm the ability for popular or genre works to contain complex self-commentary. In particular, the film's use of Harvey Keitel complicates the presumption that popular film always constructs a coherent self in its fictional characterisations.

Equally, although Ferrara's use of Madonna in the film raised criticisms about her acting "ability", it becomes clear that she (along with Keitel) has been cast precisely because she (and he) display their own personalities on-screen. Indeed, it is interesting to note that whereas Claire ultimately becomes submissive to Russell's punishment, Sarah's behaviour off-set is far more aggressive and lewd (thus replicating established press accounts of Madonna's actual personality).[12]

Arguably, critical opposition to the film was in part based on its complex and contradictory conflation of fictional roles with presumed personas. According to Richard de Cordova, film criticism unlike other modes of creative theory has frequently attempted to marginalise the aspect of *performance* that an actor brings to the role he is given.[13] As he argues in the article "Genre And Performance: An Overview", this is because it undermines presumptions about the fictional clarity that still governs critical perceptions of mainstream cinema.

By arguing that all types of popular film contain the potential for moments of performance, de Cordova draws on Jean Louis Commoli's work "Historical Fiction: A Body Too Much". This attempts to comprehend the "excessive" depiction of the body accompanying the spectacle of performance. It identifies two bodies which potentially co-exist within any one popular fictional production: the body acting (i.e. the performer) and the body acted (the fictional role being created).

As Comolli noted, in most films there remains an unproblematic fit between the two, which retards the actor's ability to step out from within the confines of his fictional role. However, in genres such as the historical film, the fit between the two is complicated by the prior existence of a real referent which becomes the criterion of judging the actor's theatrical skills[14]. In such cases, the spectator's belief shifts away from the fictional role to the actor himself and what additional skills and experiences he has brought to the performance.

Although Comolli limits himself to an analysis of performance in historical film, de Cordova extends his findings to genre cinema. He argues that popular film is also faced with the problematic split between the body acting and the body acted. By identifying genre movies as plagued by the "performative sequence", de Cordova notes:

"In those moments in films in which acting comes to the fore and is noticed, there is a split between actor and character as agents of two different actions."[15]

De Cordova notes that the only popular film format where the issue of performance has been discussed in depth is the musical. Here, the performative moment can be identified in the generic trait of the dance routine. This feature provokes a potential problem for narrative progression in that the "fictional" effect of the film is halted while the dancer/performer demonstrates his/her skills in a choreographed display.

The musical moment can therefore be defined as the point where the performer slips out of their fictional role and adds an additional dimension to the narrative. They are assisted in their performance by a number of technical and stylistic features which bracket this segment as separate from the rest of the narrative. For instance, the musical interlude is usually frontally framed, allowing performers to address the camera directly. Equally, these "disruptive scenes" are also marked by an over-emphasis on stylistic features such as camera movement and soundtrack. All of these elements become props which emphasise the elaborate nature of the actor's display, rather than fulfilling their traditional narrative role of furthering "fictional" progression.

The nature of these performances differs from production to production, but de Cordova's indication that they involve the self-reflexive utilization of film style proves important when considering **Dangerous Game**. This is because Ferrara's film is governed by a series of stylistic ambiguities which make it impossible to distinguish *his* work from the "fictional" production of Israel's that **Dangerous Game** claims to depict.

This inability to separate the differing layers of "fiction" that the film deals with is indicated in the film's pre-credit scene. Here, Ferrara eschews a traditional establishing shot in favour a frontally framed image of Israel, Maddie and their son around the dinner table. The framing of the shot, with its implication of being a film take in production, sets up an ambivalence around the use of technical and stylistic features which is carried over into the actual credit scene. Here, a black masked image track is accompanied by Israel's voice-over telling an unidentified companion to sing a rendition of the 50's rock ballad *Blue Moon* to accompany his film.[16] The composition of this credit scene and (more importantly) its link to the segment which preceded it remains unexplained, further detracting from the fictional clarity which narrative cinema seeks to construct.[17]

In the scenes which follow the film's ambiguous opening, Israel's production of *Mother Of Mirrors* does evidence a series of stylistic features which demarcate it as a "fiction in progress". Firstly, video tape technology depicts the pre-production shots of Israel's movie as separate from the rest of the narrative (which is shot on film stock). Equally, in terms of camera mounting, the conventional structure of the narrative remains separate from the jagged *vérité*, style staging which accompanies the making of *The Mother Of Mirrors*.

However, rather than assisting to bind the "fictional" component to the rest of the narrative, these stylistic features are themselves degraded once the cast of Israel's film find their lives becoming "contaminated" by the excesses of their characters' roles.[18] The subversion of these elements further indicates that performative "excess", in the words of Elizabeth Wright:

"...gets rid of the author's voice, the text's autonomy, the use of the great actor and the illusion of reality..."[19]

STANDING IN FOR JIMMY LAINE: ENUNCIATION, PERFORMANCE AND THE ACTOR AS SADISTIC DELEGATE

One scene where the clarity of the film style of **Dangerous Game** is subverted occurs in an early stage of *The Mother Of Mirrors'* pre-production

schedule. Although other key technical features make explicit Israel as the author of the film, a brief shot of a clapper-board cites "Abel Ferrara" as its director. This further heightens the ambiguity separating fact from fiction in the narrative. Its disorientating effect is also underscored by the fact that Ferrara's regular screen-play writer Nicholas Saint John is depicted as Israel's continuity assistant on set.[20]

This potential confusion between Israel and Ferrara proves a significant feature in understanding the self-reflexive logic of **Dangerous Game**. Firstly, it confirms Marshall Fine's conclusion of the close off-screen relationship which has developed between the director and Keitel. This is confirmed by the fact that Keitel saw **Bad Lieutenant** "as a kind of gift to his daughter Stella, who appears in it briefly as one of the Lt's kids".[21] This intertextual trade-off was later reciprocated by Ferrara, who cast of members of his own family in key fictional roles as Israel's relations in **Dangerous Game**.

These extensive connections between two such significant screen personas undoubtedly complicates the notion of performance discussed above. It points to the use of the actor as a stand-in or delegate enacting Ferrara's *own* desires. Effectively, this indicates a doubling of actor's transgression from the confines of his fictional role: what is being explored are *both* Keitel and Ferrara's real life concerns. Indeed, it is interesting to note that the search for redemption that drives Keitel's performances is shared in near identical fashion by Ferrara. When asked by Gavin Smith if such a spiritual quest represented the most significant aspect in his movies, the director replied:

"Of course. It's not my film, it's my life. A film is not a 90 minute thing. A film is everything that I am. We keep coming back to the point of who are we? Where do we come from? What's our future? We do plenty of dealing with the now. But I don't know how you can fucking live and not question where you're from."[22]

The duality between Ferrara and Keitel is also extended by the fact that the issues of sadism have dogged not only the actor's fictional roles (and his real life via Lorraine Bracco's claims), but also the work of the director himself. Controversially, in his earlier productions Ferrara enacted his own cinematic transgressions under the pseudonym of Jimmy Laine. In his first film **Driller Killer** (1980), he was depicted as the unbalanced artist Reno, who slaughters a variety of victims with a portable power drill. In his second film **MS 45: Angel Of Vengeance** (1981), Ferrara appears on-screen in the opening segment long enough to rape the film's heroine, and evade punishment for his actions. By casting an actor whose non-fictional interests so closely mirror his own, it leads to the potential criticism that Keitel is actually a delegate who is enacting Ferrara's own sadistic and sexual impulses by proxy.

Such a conclusion is made even more convincing by the fact that traditionally, Film Theorists such as Raymond Bellour have viewed such a close overlap between male stars and their Hollywood directors with grave suspicion. In a series of celebrated articles, Bellour outlined how Alfred Hitchcock's films replicated the director's own (sadistic) wish to scrutinise, investigate and punish the female characters he depicted.[23] For instance, in his celebrated article "Hitchcock The Enunciator" he suggested that the director used his male stars as "stand-ins" who acted out his own sadistic wishes against the women he depicted.[24]

One film that Bellour considers here, is **Marnie** (1964). In the opening sequence he argues that the spectator's perception of the female character is formed by a conjunction of the assumptions of depicted male characters with Hitchcock's cameo in the film. Importantly, the director appears briefly in the opening scene, following a conversation between Mark Rutland (Sean Connery) and Marnie's former employer Strutt. Significantly, the pair not only discuss Marnie's theft of a large sum of money from Strutt, but also her appearance (which they detail in a highly sexual manner). This immediately establishes the heroine as a figure of ambiguous morals (therefore justifying the investigation of her persona which follows), while also promoting her body as the site of sexual display for the assembled male protagonists.

In his cameo following this conversation, Hitchcock appears to validate the assumptions of these male characters by casting a look firstly at Marnie, who passes him in a hotel corridor, and then at the camera itself. Through these brief gestures, Bellour argues that Hitchcock confirms the female's body as a site of investigation and voyeurism for *both* characters and the spectator. With an intent to scrutinize, evaluate and master, these multiple gazes effect a style of visual sadism which seeks to overwhelm the heroine's defences and uncover a rationale for her behaviour. (This is actualised in the film's finale when Rutland forces Marnie to relive the repressed childhood trauma which lies at the root to her cleptomania).

Further evidence of this sadistic position appears to be given in the treatment of Marion Crane before her savage murder in **Psycho** (1960). In his analysis of this film, Bellour eschews readings that would classify Crane's treatment by Norman Bates as an aberration from the perceptions of other male characters depicted. Rather he sees the heroine as being cast as a source of erotic fascination and visual scrutiny from the point that the camera settles on her partially clad body in the film's opening scene. This sequence, which "catches" Crane and lover Sam Loomis in a post-coital situation in a cheap motel immediately cues the spectator to view her with suspicion.

The process of moral degradation is once again confirmed by Hitchcock's cameo, with the director appearing briefly outside the office where Marion works. As with the cameo from **Marnie**, Hitchcock conveys his power to "look" by briefly glancing at Marion as she enters the locale. As Bellour notes, it is significant that in his short time on-screen in this movie, the director is depicted in a white Stetson hat. This anticipates the near-identical dress sense of the Texan Jake Cassidy who Crane later encounters in the office. It is this protagonist's money that she steals as an act of revenge following his extended attempt to seduce and then survey her in a sexual manner.

Bellour's analysis of the link between the male director and the empowered actor as delegate of their "creator"'s wishes offers a persuasive interpretation of the ideological mechanisms seen to exist in mainstream film. However, as Dana Polan notes, it is premised on the assumption that Hollywood is "the ultimate briber, the ultimate concealer of codes".[25] What such a position ignores is that popular film can frequently employ certain self-reflexive methods and in so doing draw attention to their own construction. Through the use of such mechanisms, the spectator becomes divorced from the "fictional" effect that the text is attempting to produce. Simultaneously, the use of such methods challenges the view that the viewer's voyeuristic pleasure has been "elevated to a privileged unchallenged position".[26]

The importance of Polan's revision of the self-reflexive potential of popular film has relevance for considering **Dangerous Game**'s most controversial scenes. In particular, the protracted rape of Claire by Russell as

well as his revealing of near-pornographic video tape of the couple cavorting with friends threatens to tip the film into the worst excesses of male titillation/sadism.

However, in both cases, spectator awareness that they are watching

a fiction in production assists in turning these sexual scenarios into sites of displeasure. For instance, Israel's prolonged obsession in controlling the length of Claire's rape ordeal, results in looks of visible discomfort from the rest of the film crew. (One male production assistant is even ordered off-set by a female production manager for showing too much delight in the scene of sexual torture.) Equally, the erotic footage which Russell unearths as "evidence" of Claire's "degraded" lust also carries connotations of trauma, with certain shots implying that she has been forced to partake in the gathering against her will.

By constructing a film which so clearly revolves around Harvey Keitel's assumed real-life obsessions, **Dangerous Game** carries with it the elements of suffering that mark these concerns. If, as Elizabeth Wright implies, these preoccupations can be read as symptoms of an earlier (infantile) trauma, then they are referenced in the film by the reduction of the actor to a hysterical mode of gesture and display. Equally, the fact that his identity is endlessly split along a chain of characters from his own fictional role (and its delegates in *The Mother Of Mirrors*) to Abel Ferrara himself indicates an irresolvable dissolution of the self. These tensions are themselves carried over into the fiction itself, which continually halts narrative progression in favour of acts of paranoid introspection. If these features are evidence of performative hysteria, then they act through a "disturbance of the boundaries between artist and spectator, spectator and art 'object', art object and artist".[27]

NOTES

1. Elizabeth Wright, "Psychoanalysis And The Theatrical" in Patrick Campbell (ed) *Analysing Performance*, Manchester: Manchester University Press, 1996, p.176.

2. Ibid., p.175.

3. Ibid., p.176.

4. Ibid., p.183.

5. In her book *Critical Desire*, Linda Ruth Williams has further extended the comparison between psychological complaints such as hysteria and works of the creative. She notes Freud's comment (in "Totem And Taboo") which argues that the excessive gestures of the hysteric "caricature" modes of artistic representation. Williams' own comments are of importance in assessing Keitel's overblown' acting style and its possible links to the libidinal. She argues that: "Hysteria displays, gives out, puts on show a pantomime of symptoms... eventually read as external representation of internal unrest". Linda Ruth Williams, *Critical Desire*, London: Edward Arnold (1995), p.4.

6. Keitel quoted in Marshall Fine, *The Art Of Darkness*, London: Harper Collins Press, (1997), p.202.

7. Bracco cited in Marshall Fine, p.181.

8. Fine, p.202.

9. The importance of Keitel's former military training as a point of reference for his fictional roles was commented upon by Ferrara during the filming of **Bad Lieutenant**. As he noted: "He's gonna go where his character goes. He's not afraid – he's an ex-Marine, for Chrissake. He said to me when we started filming, 'My sword is sharp, my boots are shined. Just point me to the hill and I'll take it'." Abel Ferrara, cited in Marshall Fine, *The Art Of Darkness*, p.200.

10. Indeed, it is interesting that towards the end of the production Israel continues this verbal assault against Sarah in the scenes where Russell is absent.

11. Rozen, cited in Fine, p.216.

12. For an expanded account of Madonna's ability to endlessly recreate her public persona, see the section entitled "Madonna, Fashion, Image" in Douglas Kellner's book *Media Culture*, London: Routledge, (1995). Here, Kellner argues that the pop icon is also the ultimate "postmodern" symbol because: "Madonna's texts are meaning systems, which proliferate polysemic meanings and messages" (p.288). It is interesting to note that one of the key concerns which has dominated the singer's life and art is her self-confessed conflict between Catholicism and sexual desire. This split between the spiritual and the physical once again doubles Keitel's own obsessions, as well as those depicted in the fictional space of *The Mother Of Mirrors*.

13. The most extensive area research into performance theory has emerged from disciplines such as Theatre Studies. Although varied in the types of methodology applied to the concept, what this broad field of study shares is that the performer highlights the transience of identity in its social and psychological formations. Evidence of a cross-cultural analysis of this idea has been given in Richard Schechner's influential study *Between Theatre And Anthropology*, Philadelphia: University of Pennsylvania Press, (1985). Here, Schechner draws the link between the actor and the assumption of multiple roles as part of everyday activity. More recently, Marvin Carlson has studied "performance" as a feature of postmodern society. This displaces the concept of the unified self in favour of a constantly shifting construction of identity. See Carlson's *Performance: A Critical Introduction*, London: Routledge, (1996).

14. One recent film in which the gap between the historical referent and actor's skill becomes apparent is Oliver Stone's **Nixon** (1997). Here, Anthony Hopkins' rendition of the morally ambiguous political figure takes on a troubled, melancholic underpinning which befits some of the actor's wider theatrical concerns. Stone playfully exposes the gap between the real and the performative in the film's finale. Here, the affiliations that the spectator has established through Hopkins' performance are put directly at odds with the publication of Nixon's secret Watergate files, which reveal him as a racist and a bigot.

15. Richard de Cordova, "Genre And Performance: An Overview" in Barry Keith Grant (ed) *Film Genre Reader* 11, Austin: University of Texas Press, (1995), p.133.

16. The inclusion of a 50's melody in the film's opening sequence is significant, as it confirms Ferrara's use of **Mean Streets** as a frame of reference for the role he constructed around Keitel. In Scorsese's film, the use of such a musical score becomes a noticeable feature in orchestrating the bar room encounters between Charlie Cappa and his underworld associates. Ferrara had earlier parodied this movie in a scene from **Bad Lieutenant**. Here, he got Keitel to perform a naked dance routine to a soundtrack taken directly from **Mean Streets**. Once again, the complex network between Israel's role and the other characters enacted by Keitel in his career reiterates the dissolution of unified identity at the core of **Dangerous Game**.

17. It is pertinent that de Cordova identifies the moment of performance as capable of forcing a change in a text's generic direction. His comments certainly fit the ambiguity surrounding which type of Hollywood cycle Israel's movie might belong to. Although the cruel dialogues between the two protagonists are played out as a dark family melodrama, Russell's repeated forcing of Claire to address her own reflection in a broken mirror are closer to a horror movie.

18. This is most notably evident in the scene which reveals that Burns and Sarah have (briefly) become lovers off-set. Here, Russo continue to verbally abuse her in a manner identical to his fictional character. When she leaves as a result of his actions, the viewer discovers another female lover is also present in the actor's apartment. Burns' violence once again spills over from his fictional role, with him savagely beating a supply of cocaine out of her in an addictive fit which mirrors his character's drug habit. Importantly, this scene follows two sets of inter-titles detailing the pre-production stages of "L.A. rehearsals" and "principal photography" in Israel's film. The fact that the use of such technical features dissipates following Burns' outburst indicates an inability of the film's stylistic features to contain elements of performative within the depicted "fiction".

19. Elizabeth Wright, p.179.

20. Nicholas Saint John is recognisable from other cameos he has undertaken in Ferrara productions. For instance, in **MS 45: Angel Of Vengeance** he is cast as a world-weary New York cop investigating the grisly activities of the heroine/vigilante whose actions the film details. It is also significant that Zoe Tamerlis, who played this role in Ferrara's earlier film, has also held key production credits in his works. Under her trade name of Zoe Lund she scripted **Bad Lieutenant**, as well as contributing a cameo performance as a junkie who administers a fix to Keitel's character in the movie. Lund can also be spotted at a drug gathering which Israel and Sarah attend in **Dangerous Game**. Eddie's decision to attend, as well as his gradual decline, mirror the malaise afflicting Burns/Russell, further underscoring the ambiguity between persona and fictional role.

21. Cited in Fine, p.201.

22. Abel Ferrara cited in Gavin Smith, "Dealing With The Now", in Nick James (ed) *Sight And Sound*, April 1997, p.9.

23. Bellour's most famous articles include his analysis of **Psycho** "Psychosis, Neurosis And Perversion" (*Camera Obscura* 3/4 Summer 1979), and his discussion of **The Birds** (*Cahiers du Cinéma*, n. 216, October 1969). In these works he argues that the women Hitchcock depicts represent a "problem" for the narrative. This occurs because these heroines are essentially *desiring* women, whose wishes frequently threaten to dislodge the stability of the male drive underpinning the narrative. As a result, these female desires have to be "contained", a manoeuvre Hitchcock achieves by making his heroines appear transgressive or illegal. Most famously, **Psycho**'s Marion Crane is revealed as a thief (a trait shared by another of the director's noted heroine, **Marnie**). Her affair with the (technically) married Sam Loomis also casts an ambiguity over how the text positions her sexual morality. In **Vertigo** (1958), the duplicitous nature of womanhood is indicated in the figure of Madeline. She is not only engaged in an illegitimate affair with Gavin Elster, but also participates in the murder of his wife and the elaborate hoax designed to conceal events from the investigator Scottie Fergerson.

24. See Raymond Bellour. "Hitchcock The Enunciator", *Camera Obscura 2* (Fall, 1977). For a summary of Bellour's analysis see also Sandy Flitterman, "Women, Desire And The Look: Feminism And The Enunciative Apparatus In Cinema" in John Caughie (ed) *Theories Of Authorship*, London: Routledge, (1988).

25. Dana Polan, "A Brechtian Cinema? Towards A Politics Of Self-Reflexive Film" in Bill Nichols (ed) *Movies And Methods* Volume II, Berkeley: University of California Press, (1985), p.667.

26. Ibid., p.664.

27. Elizabeth Wright, p.177.

BEYOND GOOD AND EVIL:
HARVEY KEITEL IN 'THE PIANO'

Jane Campion's 1993 Cannes Palme d'Or Award winning film **The Piano**, features Harvey Keitel as George Baines, a classic anti-hero/outsider character. Set in mid-1800's "settler" New Zealand, **The Piano** tells the story of the sexual and emotional liberation of a young, dumb, Scottish woman, Ada McGrath (Holly Hunter). A love affair develops between Ada and Baines that acts as a catalyst to the process of Ada's liberation, but does not dominate the film's feminist theme of emancipation. A close examination of the film followed by a brief overview of Keitel's acting procedures, will show why Keitel is an ideal actor to play character roles which are morally ambiguous and unconventional, such as those demanded by **The Piano**.

THE STORY

The film opens with Ada's "mind thoughts"; she informs us that she has been dumb since the age of six:

"I have not spoken since I was six years old. No one knows why, not even me. My father says it is a dark talent and the day that I take it into my head to stop breathing will be my last."

We then see Ada arriving on a deserted beach in New Zealand with her nine-year-old, illegitimate child Flora (Anna Pacquin). Ada arrives in New Zealand to meet her new husband, Alisdair Stewart (Sam Neill) to whom her father has married her by long distance contract. Ada is a mail-order bride for Stewart, a first generation settler from Scotland, and small landowner. Ada has come to New Zealand because Flora's illegitimacy would otherwise condemn her to a lifetime of social exclusion in Scotland.

      Ada's boxed grand piano is also deposited on the beach with her. Ada's piano is her "voice"; without the piano to express and communicate her emotions, she is left to depend on the less immediate and indirect communication of note writing. Only Flora is able to communicate with her through sign language. Ada is therefore split into two different people[1]. Ada is the repressed Victorian female who has internalised her oppression so far that she can no longer express herself through speech, society's means of communication. Yet she is also a highly passionate pianist who has given female desire and assertion an outlet in a form where it cannot be interpreted as being in direct confrontation with the surrounding world.

      Ada and Flora spend the night camped out beneath the rigid structure of Ada's hooped crinoline cage, covered with petticoats to create a tent. In the morning, a transport party led by Stewart arrives on the beach to transport her and her possessions to his homestead which lies half a day's journey inland amongst a small Scottish settler community/mission which includes Stewart's missionary aunt. The transport party is composed of Maoris, male and female, Stewart (a *pakeha*, or white New Zealander), and Baines – who appears half-*pakeha* and half-Maori by nature of his eclectic clothing and facial tattoos. Stewart is unable to relate to Ada, his attitude is one of embarrassment, awkwardness, distance, and scrutiny. Stewart has no sense of empathy, only a desire to take command of the unknown situation. He walks over to Ada's petticoat "tent" but is too afraid to look in. His reserve is imitated by a Maori man who peers into the tent to look at Ada.

The Piano uses clothing to express both historical authenticity and character symbolism. Stewart wears clothing which is too tight, restricting his movements, a top hat which shows his status, and sombre colours, all of which serve to define his personality as being emotionally limited and conventional. Likewise both Ada and Flora wear tight black dresses, which are voluminous but restrictive and leave little room for individual expression. Baines' clothes are far more colourful and indicate the international lifestyle of an ex-whaler and traveller; his shirt is blue, of the type worn by nineteenth-century, French, livestock traders. Baines' personality is shown to be less limited than Stewart's. Baines transgresses boundaries of gender and ethnicity to identify, and emphasise, with the plight of others. If Ada and Stewart epitomize Victorian repression and defined gender roles in their appearance, then Baines offers a marked alternative.

Stewart scrutinizes Ada, he thinks of her as his object/possession, he does not speak to her directly. He pronounces her as "stunted" and asks for Baines' opinion; Baines at least looks at Ada and says with empathy, "She looks tired". Stewart decides to abandon Ada's piano and ignores her demands. Stewart cannot understand Ada's stubborn will (her "dark talent"). Baines however, does not wish for Ada to be the submissive female – although it takes a battle of wills between Ada and himself for him to understand that control over a woman will not lead to a satisfactory relationship for either of them.

Baines lives in a small, basic log cabin not far from the settlement where Ada and Stewart live. Baines is able to speak their language, and also chooses to socialise with the Maoris. The Maoris are represented as being far more flexible in their attitudes social and gender roles. In one scene we see Baines bathing by the river with his Maori friends, who talk in very frank terms about sexuality. They also accept the "camp" behaviour of a Maori man and joke about his effeminacy and the masculinity of one of the women. This is a far cry from Stewart's world of gentle enquiries from his aunt, and

suppressed murmurs about Ada's lack of "affection". Baines offers a path to the transgression of Victorian social conventions and gender roles. This presents Ada with the opportunity and support to become less alienated from herself. Baines offers Stewart eighty acres of land in return for Ada's piano, and lessons with Ada in his cabin.

Ada and Baines eventually fall in love during passionate "flesh-bargaining" piano lessons. Baines attempts to seduce Ada by bargaining with her for the return of her piano. They barter for possession of the black keys of the piano; the number of keys exchanged varies according to the acts which he wishes her to undertake. Initially this involves watching Ada play in increasing states of undress, it then moves on to touching Ada's clothes, parts of her exposed flesh, and then to undressing himself and requesting that Ada lies naked on his bed with him. The ultimate climax to this arrangement is cut short by Baines' dislike of what he considers to be a merely commercial exchange, whereby he is left feeling that Ada does not love him, and that she is becoming a "whore".

Baines is at odds with the patriarchal system and Victorian values represented by Stewart and the other *pakeha* settlers. He is considered to be a heathen partly due to the fact that he cannot read or write. This excludes Baines from the power dynamics of society, where the ability to speak and communicate with authority is crucial. The other settlers make fun of Baines' lack of education. Ada objects to his ownership of her piano because "He's an oaf, he can't read, he's ignorant". Ada is also excluded from social authority by her own lack of speech. The notes that she writes in the small silver notebook tied round her neck are less authoritative than direct speech because their presentation is delayed and indirect.

Baines and Ada identify with each other on some level, both choosing ways to make their lives more satisfying outside of the social order which oppresses them. For Ada this comes initially from Flora and her piano; Baines is drawn to the music and to her own "outsider" stance. Music offers Ada and Baines an alternative language of emotion and thought, which cannot so easily be pinned down to a particular interpretation. Likewise, Baines is able to empathise with the Maoris; he speaks their disempowered language both figuratively and literally. This makes him a useful go-between for the land grabbing *pakehas* such as Stewart. Baines is willing to cooperate with Maori cultural beliefs and understands their anger and frustration regarding their exploitation. In effect, because of his own partial exclusion from the other settlers, by nature of his lower place on the social rung, Baines is able to identify with the lack of power and desires of the social "other" – the "dispossessed". This is an attribute which enables Ada to be treated as his equal rather than as submissive. Ada can then allow herself to fall happily in love, and at the end of the film we see her social appearance beginning to merge with her hidden emotional desires when she leaves with Baines and Flora for a new life, and begins to speak again.

THE THEME – COLONISATION

The theme of **The Piano** reaches beyond that of a love story which joins together two social outsiders, enabling them to become more "at one" with themselves. The theme of **The Piano** is essentially that of colonisation. For the central metaphor, Ada's piano, represents the objectification and male exchange of female desire and expression. Also, colonisation in the wider

sense of female, and ethnic oppression in the expansionist Victorian age. **The Piano** forces the audience to see the wider implications of what might initially appear to be just a battle over the ownership of a piano. It also allows a comparison to be drawn between historical themes and contemporary situations. The nineteenth century presents ready-made and very powerful symbolism by which to represent colonisation and repression of both women and various social and "ethnic" groups. Such acts were easier to "see"; gender and ethnic difference appear less obvious in the contemporary world where communication and technology now colonise, but they still exist and the act of colonisation remains as persistent as ever.

When Ada first arrives on the beach at New Zealand, she is seen to pull back a broken plank from the piano's box, insert her hand and gently caress the keys of the long silent piano. Ada attempts to colonise her own desire and expression through her music and piano; it is part of her. She has defensively withdrawn this part of herself from the world around her to prevent its "contamination" and misrepresentation; she guards it fiercely but treats it with the utmost respect. Her act of colonisation is one of retaliation and protection causing both self-alienation, and social exclusion. It causes her voice to become displaced, fragmented and incoherent, requiring an effort of interpretation from those around her. This is similar to the position of the

Maoris whose language and actions become misinterpreted when observed by the *pakehas*.

The issue of language is also one of colonisation. Language is a construct that produces a hierarchical system of naming, possession, and meaning. It is a system of authority and exchange where power is invested in those given the authority of being able to possess their own name and name others[2]. Exclusion from this form of colonisation is effective on every level. Stewart on the other hand is represented as the violent face of colonisation. He tries to empower himself by taking from another, whether Ada or Maori. This form of colonisation raises issues of possession and conflict. The Maoris' land, like Ada's piano, becomes a possession to be bartered over. Abstention or denial of the power invested in language offers escapism rather than opposition. Ada's music may offer her, and Baines, an outlet from repression but it does not offer a way to confront the world of Stewart.

Ada's piano, like the Maoris' land, is seen by the men around her as being there for the taking. Stewart literally tries to rape Ada both by selling her piano to Baines and then twice in person when he discovers that she is having an affair with Baines (he watches them have sex through "peepholes" in the walls and floor of Baines' cabin). Stewart's first attempt at rape is in the forest. The hoops of Ada's dress restrict her movement and she gets caught in the undergrowth, but they also prevent Stewart from being able to get close to her[3]. The second rape attempt occurs after Stewart has chopped off Ada's finger in retaliation of her attempt to see Baines again. This time Ada's will, her fevered stare, prevents Stewart from taking advantage of her.

Like her piano, Ada is always an object to Stewart – something which he must own, rather than hold joint ownership with. She serves to reflect his glory and anything that she owns must service his desires. Ada's piano represents a distorted picture of independence because it has no authority or power, it remains as a silent object of desire because neither Stewart or Baines have use for it in terms of their own desires to make it play, to give it "voice". Stewart is quite happy to part with it although Baines is aware of, and comes to respect, the importance that it holds for Ada.

Stewart likewise will not accept the authority of the Maoris' language and the legitimacy of their claim to land. He treats them like children offering them blankets, buttons, and then guns for their land. He cannot understand how or why they have the right to land which they do not view in terms of possession, but instead see in terms of ancestral and sacred land which must remain unused. Stewart needs to have everything marked out in black and white terms, in the same way that his land must be mapped-out. Stewart himself may not appear to be a very effective coloniser in the sense that the Maoris mock him, his wife disobeys him, and Baines has an affair with her.

Yet Stewart's difficulties show how colonisation is a construct enforced by brutality, repression and fear rather than a natural right.

Ada, and her piano (repressed sexuality) are objects to be scrutinized by the men around them. Ada is always being peered at and poked by men: when she shelters on the beach beneath her petticoats; through the lens of a camera when Stewart sets up their "wedding" photograph; by Stewart when she has sex with Baines; by Baines when he pokes his finger through a hole in her stocking during their "piano lessons"; and so on. The piano itself is likewise caressed by Baines in Ada's absence. The Victorians placed "socks" over the legs of inanimate objects such as pianos, tables, chairs and so on because these objects were felt to be indecent, in other words they offered displaced sexual arousal to the sexually repressed who were unable to see the "real thing". The piano's sexual surrogacy is reinforced by the appearance of a blind piano tuner. The piano tuner can no longer see objects of desire. He is reduced to sniffing and caressing the piano. However, unlike Stewart, Baines is willing for Ada to see him unclothed, to become an object to her.

The Piano can be seen as questioning colonisation beyond the confines of the cinema screen into the wider context of film making. Ada is trying to repossess her independence by taking ownership first of her piano (her surrogate voice) and then her actual speaking voice. In the same manner both the audience and the film makers have undertaken a voyeuristic contract to re-assess the historical and contemporary repression, primarily of women but also of less empowered social and ethnic groups. **The Piano** reclaims a representational heritage for women. It centres on a historical period of extreme repression and seeks to show how a woman could become disempowered and then re-empowered.

The film uses costume in the film to show that social identity is constructed, built up in layers rather than being expressive of individuality. For example, Ada is shown to wear her wedding dress as a costume. She wears her rigid black dress beneath it, and beneath that her white underclothes. Ada is not actually marrying Stewart, neither is she a virgin, she is acting, representing marriage for a post, non-event photograph. The wedding photograph is a representation of a constructed symbol. This use of costume and representation offers an effective way of showing that appearances are deceptive and constructed for a purpose. Such costume layering and role playing also undermines such rigid social stereotypes such as virgin/whore, for all roles are constructed to serve short-lived socially descriptive purposes. This is emphasized in the film by a theatrical production of Bluebeard where Flora is seen wearing an angel costume, and then betrays her mother by telling Stewart that Ada is still trying to communicate with Baines. She shows him a "love letter", an engraved piano key that Ada has torn from the piano.

Flora temporarily plays the role of the patriarchal guardian because her mother has not been communicating with her.

Literary texts published around the time when the film is set were unable to offer such insights or solutions. This was due to different reasons: lack of access to publishing (many women wrote under male pseudonyms), unpopular reception of "feminist" viewpoints, and lack of financial and social alternatives for women. This lack of equality was reflected in the often unconvincing, "quick-fix" solutions of romantic texts such as Charlotte Bronte's *Jane Eyre* (1847), where the heroine, Jane, can only find equality with the symbolically "castrated" Mr. Rochester. Rochester has been physically and psychologically disempowered in an accident caused by his "mad" wife.[4]

The Piano does not have to resort to "quick-fix" solutions because neither Baines nor Ada have to undergo rapid character transformations in order to respect each other. Baines is supportive of Ada's independence. Yet he does not always understand her, and overprotects her instead of immediately accepting her own desires, but life with Baines is undeniably better than life with Stewart. At the end of the film Baines, Ada and Flora leave for a new life in Nelson after Stewart chops off Ada's finger. Ada's piano is loaded onto a large Maori canoe. She asks that the piano to be thrown overboard, Baines insists that the piano is balanced and of no danger to themselves or the crew. He tells her that he has the "love letter" that she sent him, "I've been given the key, I'll have it mended". One of the Maori boatmen agrees with Ada's request. He says the piano is a "coffin", it is Ada's dead voice, her surrogate voice which displaces her desire and sexuality. Ada needs to get rid of this dead voice in order that she can learn to speak again with a living voice. The piano is thrown overboard; Ada is pulled over with it because she places her foot amongst the ropes that hold it. She chooses to fight for her life.

"What a death!
What a chance!
What a surprise!
My will has chosen life!
Still, it has had me spooked, and many others besides."

Baines makes Ada a metal finger, and she becomes a piano teacher in Nelson. At the end of the film, Ada can be seen as having become attuned to society. She has a new piano, but it is her means of living and pleasure, not her voice.

HARVEY KEITEL

The convincing resolution to **The Piano** owes much to the casting of Harvey Keitel as George Baines. Keitel is not a traditional star in the Hollywood sense. His talent is to become whoever he is portraying, to merge with the character to the point of personal invisibility. Keitel is a practitioner of the Method school of acting. He grew up in the early fifties admiring directors such as Kazan and Cassavetes, and actors such as Marlon Brando and James Dean. He followed in their footsteps by attending the Actor's studio in New York, studying the "Method" with Stella Adler, Frank Corsaro and Lee Strasberg. Keitel involved himself in an acting style which submerges the actor's personality through attempting to live and behave as the character being portrayed. This is a transgressive view of identity that attempts to close the gap between self and "other". This form of acting suits the ideology of low-budget, independent film production, which often highlights political and social discontent. **The Piano** can be seen in this light; it was relatively low budget, its director and producers were women, and its theme incorporates social and identity politics.

Keitel has always been a supporter of this side of the film industry and has worked with directors who are prepared to push beyond stereotypical character portrayal. For example in Martin Scorsese's **Mean Streets** (1973), Keitel plays the character Charlie, who not unlike Baines, hovers over the boundary between social acceptance and exclusion. Like Baines, Charlie has finds himself attracted to the social "other", his character is complex and contradictory, and partly grew from improvised acting on set with Robert De Niro. Keitel has the skill and physical appearance to allow a character's behaviour to seem unpredictable; he can easily appear brutal or empathetic. This is partly the reason that Keitel often plays good or bad characters or those who hover between the two.

Keitel as able to present Baines as a person who is open to possibility and change. The character of Baines could have easily been seen as a rather racist reworking of Shakespeare's Caliban, like an international traveller who identifies with the "other" for a short time but then returns to colonial costume. At the end of the film Baines is simply no longer noticeable as a white European with Maori tattoos, he has become merely himself.

NOTES

1. Split personality effects, especially in women, are common features in Victorian texts. However these "split" personalities were translated into rather more colourful representations such as madness and supernatural possession, than the actual symptoms of "hysteria"/psychological disorders focusing on visibility and identity, for example eating disorders. For a fuller overview see Stella Bruzzi, "Jane Campion: Costume Drama And Reclaiming Women's Past", in Cook, P & Dodds, P. (eds.), *Women And Film: A Sight And Sound Reader*. Scarlet Press, 1993. (1st pub. *Sight & Sound*, Vol. 3, no. 10, Oct. 1993.)

2. The power invested in language in the West is termed as "phallogocentricism" by the French philosopher, Jacques Derrida. Essentially, it means that the authority to name and name others is a patriarchal, and hierarchical, scheme. This means that white men have historically been seen as having the power to impose their name on others by erasing all former names. For example, on the slave plantations of the American South during the last century, each slave had their own name either taken away, or given to them, by their master. Each slave was given the surname (patriarchal name), of their master irrelevant of whether they were actually related in any way. The surname represented ownership, the loss of the right of self-identification. This use of language obviously has overtones in the context of gender and marriage. (See also Adele Olivia Gladwell, *Catamania: A History Of The Female Voice*, p.235–242. Creation Books, 1995.)

3. See Stella Bruzzi.

4. An interesting comparison can be made to Nathaniel Hawthorne's *The Scarlet Letter* (1850), recently filmed by Roland Joffé. Set in 17th century Puritan New England, it tells a similar story to that of **The Piano**, but its heroine Hester Prynne forces those around her to reinterpret her "sinful" behaviour. However, like **The Piano**, it does not suggest that society can suddenly accept women as equals.

CHOCOLATE MILK:
HARVEY KEITEL IN 'CLOCKERS'

The titles for Spike Lee's **Clockers** (1995) are presented against a gruesome montage of police pathology photographs showing exit wounds and darkly gleaming pools of blood, spliced together with strips of black and yellow incident tape. All the faces are black. Ghetto murals show elaborate memorial portraits and wall-sized cartoon images of kids packing guns. Heavily stylized, they are followed closely by a detail of a newspaper front page bearing the headline "Toy Gun – Real Tragedy".

Having laid out the scenery, it's time for Lee to bring on his main character Strike, played by Mekhi Phifer, who strides with easy confidence onto a slightly raised dais, located in the middle of a Brooklyn park square, a flag pole at its centre. He looks as if he were stepping onto a stage, except he has been giving nothing to say. Instead he smiles softly at the camera. No lines to deliver.

Based on the novel by Richard Price, who also wrote the original screenplay, **Clockers** had a rather fractured time of it getting made. Originally Martin Scorsese was to have directed the film, but then dropped out after **Casino** claimed his attention. When Lee took over the project, he rewrote the script, altering its focus. Where Price had made homicide detective Rocco Klein the protagonist of *Clockers*, Lee opted for small-time drug hustler Strike, whom Klein suspects of having gunned down a rival dealer. Effectively turning the whole narrative inside out, Lee's version of **Clockers** concentrates not upon the investigation of a crime but the meaning that crime has for the community in which it takes place. In other words, the didactic wins out over the procedural, and Harvey Keitel, as Detective Klein, isn't left with a whole lot to do. Except perhaps take some sharp lessons in the political economy of the soul as this overwrought ideological melodrama unfolds.

In the same tradition of blue collar American writers such as Hubert Selby Jr and Nelson Algren, Price explores the grim poetry and nightmarish certainties of modern inner-city living. His is a world in which ambition easily decays into an uneasy complacency. Earlier novels include his 1974 street gang classic *The Wanderers*, made into a movie by Walter Hill in 1979; *Blood Brothers*; *Ladies Man*; and *The Breaks*.

"Richard Price," the *Washington Post* once wrote, "is to fiction what Martin Scorsese is to film." He even wrote the screenplay for Scorsese's epic meditation on hard work, hustling and self-worth, **The Color Of Money** (1986).

Spike Lee takes Price's restless economics of social identity and transposes them onto the drug-dealing community of **Clockers** with alarming

results. This is political cinema for the Jerry Springer generation. While Klein and his colleagues circle and probe, Lee focuses upon the three key relationships in Strike's life, all of which are with men.

The first up is Rodney Little, played by Delroy Lindo, the main dealer for whom Strike is clocking. Rodney runs a candy store, which acts as a front for his various operations, but he keeps Strike working from the benches ranged around the Brooklyn park square, directing a small crew of homies to make the drops and pick up the money while he keeps watch ("clocks") for the inevitable police raids. The strain of such constant nervous vigilance has severely affected Strike's stomach, rendering him incapable of keeping anything down but Chocolate Moo, a milky brown slop which he is constantly shown sucking straight from the bottle. Rodney wants Strike to kill a fellow clocker, Daryl Adams, who runs Ahab's, a local junk food restaurant. In return for whacking Daryl, Strike can take his place flipping burgers and dealing drugs from the warmth and safety of Ahab's formica and chrome interior. Rodney also knows that he can let the Chocolate Moos do Strike's thinking for him and that Daryl is consequently as good as dead.

Meanwhile, Strike's brother Victor, played with gracefully controlled intensity by Isaiah Washington, is also having trouble with his digestion. Holding down two jobs to keep together a family whom he rarely sees, Victor has become physically sick from working shifts at Hambones, a rival fast-food restaurant. He is first seen in the corner of a noisy bar, brooding over a beer, while Strike spins him some tale of how Daryl Adams, over at Ahab's, hits on little girls and needs to be popped. Does he know anyone who could handle that sort of thing?

A working stiff and church-goer, dedicated to getting his wife and kids out of the projects and into a better life, Victor appears to represent everything that Strike is not. Despite remaining close as brothers, a world of expectations separates the two men. Victor has old-fashioned blue collar aspirations, while all Strike really wants is to get off those fucking benches. It's the difference between beer and chocolate milk.

Also seen slurping down the Moos is Tyrone, a fatherless kid from the neighbourhood, played by Pee Wee Love, who looks up to Strike and seeks to emulate him, despite his mother's best efforts and dire warnings. A strapping figure of angry street-theatre decency, Tyrone's mom would be totally at home as one of Oprah's guests, animatedly confronting pushers on "My kids respect the local dealer". Having no real contact with his own mother, and, with no father in sight either, Strike's family has been replaced by the all-male triumvirate of Rodney, Victor and Tyrone, each of whom turns out to be guilty of murder. Time for Detective Klein to make an entrance.

DOUBLE WHALE ON A BUN

Rocco Klein is a man of excellent appetites. The first time we see him, he's cramming the last remains of a fast-food snack into his mouth as he and his partner drive over to Ahab's burger joint to visit the scene of the crime. Rocco and partner Larry (John Turturro) both distance themselves from the worlds of chocolate milk and beer. It's a Saturday night, and they prefer to swig vodka from airline miniatures, then fling the bottles out of their patrol car window. What the hell, it provides low-income job opportunities for the local community. However, when Larry mutters "mazeltof" to Rocco before drinking, it becomes clear that some difference is being acknowledged between the two cops. Only the most vestigial traces of Klein's Jewish-Italian identity remain from Price's original story in Lee's version. No longer a central concern, they become almost camouflaged beneath the exchange of casual racial epithets that occur whenever the cops show. The concerns and convictions behind Keitel's portrayal of Klein remain unexamined as a result, giving his performance a curiously suspended quality throughout.

Whatever deep game Rocco Klein is playing with himself, as he eases his way through the crowd, it stays well below the surface. This does not prevent him from participating in the grotesque comedy scene taking place outside Ahab's, where the cops are cracking jokes over the murder victim's body as they search for exit and entry wounds.

"Bing, bing, bing. Ricochet rabbit," he raps out in clipped, unfussy tones, indicating a bullet's trajectory through flesh and bones.

Bringing a brisk, formal energy to Klein's remarks, Keitel suggests a man who has not been soured by his experiences but who one has allowed himself to become hardened towards pointless observance of details.

He's got a job to do, and he gets off on every second of it. While the blood and brains continue to ooze out onto the asphalt, accompanied by an uninterrupted stream of smart-ass one-liners, Larry recognizes the deceased as Daryl Adams, who used to work at Rodney's candy store before moving on to manage Ahab's. Up above them, on the burger bar roof, a vast pink and white whale spouts useless clouds of smoke from its neon blow hole. Unfortunately, detectives like Klein don't believe in such signs and portents. Not when they've just found some clear plastic wraps filled with drugs in one of Daryl Adams' pockets, making him a clocker in their eyes and thus narrowing down the field of inquiry more than somewhat.

Or maybe it doesn't. Drugs exist in **Clockers** as a form of generic white-powder Moby Dick. They don't just make you crazy, but everyone else as well. In a society where only the cops have real jobs, you are what you choose to stick in your face. Spike Lee presents a community where junk rules the standard conduits of consumption from the corner store to the trash can. The American dream for the likes of Strike and Daryl is to deal drugs and burgers at the same time. Dead bodies in the parking lot are just an economic by-product. Surplus value. No wonder Klein is repeatedly shown handing out business cards to every potential witness he encounters.

When Strike's brother Victor subsequently turns himself over to the police after church on Sunday, claiming that he was the one who shot Adams after an altercation outside Ahab's, Klein refuses to believe it.

He won't even cuff the guy. "We locked up the wrong brother," he tells his partner Larry, who frankly couldn't care less so long as someone goes down for the slaying. Klein, meanwhile, encourages Victor to plead self-defence, convinced that he's taking the heat for his brother.

Having gone for beer over chocolate milk, Klein's belief that Victor's confession is a case of misguided decency soon curdles into the unshakable assumption that he's being played for a fool. "What I want to know," Klein fumes, "is how these two yo's get the balls big enough to think they can put this one past me?" Good question.

REAL GUN – TOY TRAGEDY

"Nintendo or Sega?" Klein's partner Larry asks Tyrone when the two cops first encounter him in one of the project's elevators. "Sega," is the immediate reply. Larry isn't just passing the time by talking about the elaborate VR visor and console set which the kid's toting. He's also establishing the boy's age and frame of reference. Sega demographics have always tended to be a shade older than those for Nintendo. In other words, Tyrone is moving on to more grown-up games. Thanks to Strike, he's playing a virtual reality shoot 'em up that exactly replicates not only the Brooklyn park square, with its flag pole and its benches, but also the murder which Tyrone will soon commit. Tyrone's answer has already told Larry as much. His next two questions are about gangsters and guns. Adulthood and maturity have no place in the criminal neverland which Strike and his homeboys have created for themselves out on the benches.

Thanks to the exchange rate mechanism operating in this garden of urban delights, dealing has become a form of sexualized transaction which expresses itself through childish obsessions. Strike plays with an elaborate toy train set at home, while his homie, Scientific, endlessly discusses gats and shootings with the rest of the group. Violent death advertises itself everywhere as a series of games and displays. A TV in a crowded bar shows rappers brandishing handguns at the camera, while young kids clap their hands and make up rhymes about gunning people down.

Gunplay runs like a sexual current between the male characters, transforming all bodily contact into snarling shows of aggression. Men can hardly stand to touch each other. Dealers are repeatedly shown handing drugs over to female customers but will use only the most indirect methods when passing them along to other males. Cops frisk dealers by getting them to drop their pants and then reaching under their crotches from behind. Any money they find is then tauntingly thrown to the gangs of watching children. "These cuffs are tight," Strike complains to a local black cop who is taking him in for questioning. "You and I use to be tight," the cop simpers in reply.

"What'll you do for me?" Klein is asked when making a deal with a narcotics agent. "Nothing you don't do for yourself," Klein snaps back.

Rodney establishes his dominance over Strike by forcing a gun barrel between his lips and calling him a bitch, while the threat of homosexual rape or male penetration is constantly referred to or joked about.

"Have I treated you like an erection?" an aggrieved Klein asks Strike during an unofficial interrogation on the street. At the same time, Victor is well on his way to becoming a correctional facility punk.

"Some of these men love jail," he announces in a stunned, disbelieving voice, after someone steals his sneakers and his face is slashed with a razor.

This dark unreconstructed world of dreams and nightmares even comes with its very own boogie man. An old junky pal of Rodney's who is dying of AIDS, Errol Barnes is a shambling gothic cartoon of a man, muttering curses and bugging his eyes in the shadows. Once a stone killer, he's now too strung out to do more than give Strike dirty looks and terrorize little kids

like Tyrone. Meanwhile, the drugs continue to work. Like a demented Ahab, Klein remains intent upon pursuing the wrong whale.

"You did it!" he shouts, confronting Strike in a tense scene set outside precinct headquarters. "I know it. You know it. Your brother knows it... he probably thinks that he's doing the decent thing here."

Keitel's depiction of inflamed righteousness, however, has been given nothing to work against. Whatever there is in Klein's personal make-up capable of responding so strongly to the individual fates of these two brothers, Spike Lee's film offers it very little with which to connect.

All that's left for Keitel to exploit is Klein's barely concealed disgust at Strike's childish consumption of chocolate milk. It represents a snotty youthful challenge to his masculine notions of authority. "I can read you like a Marvel Spiderman comic book," he rages. "I've been inside your bald pea-brain since you were born. Twenty fucking years! You don't play *me*! I play *you*!" The camera focuses in tight on Keitel, but there's nowhere left for the scene to go. When Larry finally tells Rocco to calm down, his voice sounds as if it were coming from a different film.

NOVUS ORDO SECLORUM

The truth is that Victor has been the right brother all along; a hard-working family man who had one beer too many that night and killed a man after his feelings of rage and frustration became too much to bear. Strike had merely singled Daryl Adams out as the one to die. The shooting unites the two brothers still further in sickness. We are shown Victor back home after the murder, vomiting into the toilet bowl while confessing the crime to his mother, who has remained silent about his guilt until things start looking really bad for her younger son, Strike. Klein's reaction to this revelation is an unexpected one.

Rather than ask himself where Victor's mom got the balls to think she could get that past him or trade his badge in for a guest spot on Ricki Lake talking about how "We All Feel The Need To Kill", he helps another mother dummy up for her son.

Peddling furiously on the new bicycle which Strike has bought him, Tyrone goes speeding up to Errol at the entrance to the park square and shoots him in the chest with Strike's gun. The scene is a blood-spattered reconstruction of the one played out on Tyrone's VR games console, the only differences being that the formula "Gat'cha" doesn't appear in the sky above Errol's lifeless body and there are way too many witnesses this time. When the boy gets wheeled into the station house, however, Klein is there to give his take on events.

Encouraging both mother and son to lie about what has happened, Klein constructs a fantasy scenario in which Tyrone finds the gun in some bushes, hangs onto it so he can act tough in front of the other boys, then uses it to shoot child-molesting old AIDS junkie Errol in self-defence. In an absurdly overblown sequence, Keitel appears as a life-sized digital sprite in a pop video reenactment of what he now describes as having officially happened. Paced like an MTV public information slot, it shows Keitel zipping along beside Tyrone on his bike while the benches fill up with a choreographed chorus line of homeboys waving guns at each other in a wildly exaggerated manner.

Thanks to the rapid editing, coupled with Keitel's incessant, hectoring narrative, Tyrone is presented as a frightened hysteric caught up in a blur of events beyond his control. By ignoring the fact Tyrone has already rehearsed the scene on his Sega console or that he was actually trying to prevent Errol from killing Strike, Klein's version of events contributes still further to the universe of collapsing values and fake exchanges in which Lee has set his film.

Klein may be incapable of dealing with truth as a homicide detective, but he's not alone in his deficiency. Priests hand over murderers at the altar in this movie, while caring mothers raise good sons to be killers. No one can

do their job any more. There's no pay back. Even the drug dealers don't get to see that much money up close. It hardly has a presence at all. The stuff they're pushing won't make you high either.

"This shit is like truth serum," Rodney gloats savagely while describing the effects of crack cocaine upon his clientele, and Spike Lee seems set upon proving he's right with an almost nihilistic singleness of purpose. Firmly gripped in the psychic choke-hold of narcotics, truth and justice, family and religion, friendship, youth and culture are exposed as an empty collection of hollow jokes and bitter asides. Lee doesn't leave his audience with many soft options.

In persuading Strike to shoot Adams for him, Rodney appeals to him as a brother, dazzles him with visions of himself as a biblical avenger, then finally dangles Adams' job in front of him as a reward. The guy comes over sounding like Martin Luther King, Dale Carnegie and Ronald McDonald all rolled into one. He also gets the other kids in the neighbourhood going with his high-motivation salesman's pitch, encouraging them to hold out their hands and watch the accumulation of cash turn them green.

When Strike reminds Rodney of their deal, however, he retreats to plain, old-fashioned Social Darwinism: "I didn't say nothing to you about shooting nobody. I said, you want Daryl's spot, you get it for yourself."

That's middle management for you. The days of manual endeavour and earning a crust by the sweat of your brow have long since gone, shrunk down to the train set Strike fusses over. In driving him to the railway station, Klein may be offering him the chance to trade up his toy engines for the opportunity to ride on a real one, but it's the false lure of nostalgia that informs the choice. Having passed his trains on to Tyrone as replacements for the VR visor and his gun, the young boy is heard echoing Sprite's history of the American railways as he watches them going in endless circles round the miniature track. It's a lecture on the past Tyrone is giving, not the present.

The future, meanwhile, remains in doubt. There's not so much a bleak reverence for the dignity of labour pervading the whole movie, but the even bleaker awareness that a drug-derived economy is no substitute in its absence. With clocking or a McJob as the only options for survival, and professional law enforcement essentially a joke, who polices the ghetto in such straitened times? What order of economic activity can still be trusted? With its MTV soundtrack of rap and soul tunes, elaborate pop video stylings and digitized computer graphics, **Clockers** offers the possibility that the new urban space belongs to those who can manipulate people, information and images the most effectively. People who understand the media and how it works. People like Spike Lee perhaps.

HARVEY KEITEL DISAPPEARS IN 'FROM DUSK TILL DAWN'

Robert Rodriguez's 1995 film, **From Dusk Till Dawn**, opens in the Texan desert, somewhere near the border of Mexico. Two brothers Richie (Quentin Tarantino) and Seth Gecko (George Clooney) are terrorizing the customers and token staff member at a general store. Richie is clearly trigger-happy and recklessly creates a shoot-out in the store, in which he is wounded. As the two brothers leave the store it explodes into a ball of flame, but they are so deep in argument that they do not appear to notice. They climb into their car, the trunk of which contains a terrified hostage from a bank raid the brothers have recently completed.

Role credits.

The Gecko's are heading south, towards Mexico, and El Ray, a place in which, for 30% of their booty, they can make their home. Near the border the brothers hide out at a motel, where Richie brutally slays the kidnapped bank teller. Seth, drinking beer in the motel's parking lot, is nearly hit by a large rambler. Driven by the (recently?) widowed Minister, Jacob (Harvey Keitel), who – having lost his faith – is taking a road trip with his two children Katie (Juliette Lewis) and Scott (Ernest Liu).

The brothers hijack the mobile home, and force the family to drive them across the border to their destination, a suitably exaggerated biker and trucker bar called the Titty Twister. Following a brief, and violent, confrontation with the doorman (one of three small cameos played by Richard Marin, a.k.a. "Cheech"), the group enters the sleazy bar.

A grim truce between the two families emerges in the bar, dictated by Seth who states that, as long as the ex-Minister and his children remain in the Titty Twister until dawn, when his connection, Carlos, arrives to take the Gecko's to El Ray, everything will be fine. As Seth observes, the (relative) stasis will be maintained as long as both families maintain an "I don't fuck with you, you don't fuck with me attitude". The stand off appears to be working, when the bar's hostess, the suitably named Santanico Pandemonium (Salma Hayek) appears and performs an exotic/erotic dance. Following the completion of the dance the doorman – having recovered enough from his beating to raise trouble – attacks Richie. Following a brief and violent altercation, the two brothers shoot the doorman. However Richie's hand – recently wounded in the shoot out in the store – is wounded yet again, when a knife impales it to the wooden table top at which he is sitting, spilling his blood in a slick across the table. At the sight of this blood Santanico transforms into a monstrous vampire and attacks Richie.

As if on cue the entire bar-staff, house-band, and dancing girls

transform into vampires and attack the clientele. Following a bloody battle, all who remain standing are Seth, Jacob, Katie, Scott, and two of the bar's biker clients, played by Tom Savini and Fred Williamson. Whilst the vampires amass outside the barricaded bar Jacob is forced to reconsider his faith, and the embattled survivors are gradually slain in a series of violent vignettes. Finally only Katie and Seth remain, and are about to be killed by the legions of vampires when the sun rises, killing the vampires as they enter its rays, the light streaking through the bullet holes in the bar's shuttered windows. Carlos arrives and breaks open the door to the bar, sending more light into the building. Seth and Katie escape, Seth heading to El Ray with Carlos, and Katie left standing in the bar's parking lot. As the film ends the audience sees the back of the bar, which appears to be an ancient temple; surrounding it is the skeletal remains of dozens of trucks and bikes, suggesting that the vampires at the Titty Twister have been feeding off the bloody corpses of travellers for a long time.

Superficially **From Dusk Till Dawn** appears to be two genre films joined together, one half getaway movie and one half splatter movie. As the film moves from one genre to the next – with the arrival of the group at the Titty Twister – the film's narrative subverts the text's status. Whilst the first section of the film eschewed direct references to the film's ontological status as film, the second section opens with the bar's doorman describing the kind of "pussy" to be found within. As he reaches the end of his sophomoric sexism, which is shot from below, positioning the audience's gaze as looking up to him, he bends down and directly addresses the camera/gaze/audience. In doing this the film deconstructs its own verisimilitude, and announces its move to a different method of storytelling. Whilst this cinematic gesture announces a new form of narrative, it should of course be noted that, despite the narrative emphasis on realism in the opening scenes, the first section of the film was equally as fantastical, with the apparently bullet proof Richie managing to only get wounded in a hail of bullets, with the absurd luck of the border crossing, Seth's prison breakout (about which the audience are only obliquely told), and so forth.

Throughout both sections of the film there is an overriding narrative emphasis on the confrontation between families. In the first part of the film the two families are those of Jacob et al and the Gecko brothers, whilst in the second section – allied by an uneasy truce – the two (human) families fight the vampires. The vampires are, as the film makes clear, the spawn of evil, and thus exist in some symbiotic familial relationship with one another. A relationship spread by blood and saliva, each corpse reviving as yet another soulless vessel of evil. Notably all the family groups are devoid of mothers, the brothers existing as a self-contained entity, with Richie's psychosis held in place by his devotion to the paternal figure of Seth. Jacob's wife, and the mother of his children, has died in a car crash, and the vampire's Mistress is killed by the humans.

Genre films are defined largely by the audience's familiarity with the accoutrements and narrative devices which pertain to that specific genre, whilst **From Dusk Till Dawn** manipulates (or at least attempts to) the audience's expectations, it demands a knowledge of textual metanarrative and signifying practices in order that the audience is able to decode its pleasures. Characters in **From Dusk Till Dawn** are generic stereotypes: the religious figure who has lost his faith, the killer who becomes a hero, the innocent girl who survives[1], and the sexually sadistic vampire. Thus **From Dusk Till Dawn** references similar siege-based horror films such as **The Evil Dead** (Sam Raimi, 1983), **Night Of The Living Dead**, **Dawn Of The Dead** and **Day Of The Dead**, (George Romero, 1968, 1978, and 1985 respectively), possession movies such as, once again, **The Evil Dead** trilogy, and vampire movies such as **Near Dark** (Kathryn Bigelow, 1987); as well as films such as **The Getaway** (Sam Peckinpah, 1972), **Gun Crazy** (Joseph H. Lewis, 1949), and Tarantino's own **Reservoir Dogs** (1992). The methods by which genre films function is acknowledged within the diagesis of **From Dusk Till Dawn**, primarily via the film's repeated references to other cinematic texts, an element which the film's script-writer and producer,

Quentin Tarantino, has made – at least in part – his trademark[2]. In **From Dusk Till Dawn** the film's intertextuality is signified not just by the audience's expectations of the conventions of the genre/s, but also by the deliberate signifiers to other texts positioned within the mise-en-scène, such as the Scott's tee-shirt which bares the slogan "Precinct 13", referring to the John Carpenter movie **Assault On Precinct 13** (1976), in which a police station is surrounded by vengeful gangs anxious to kill the few inhabitants – a group of convicts and policemen unified by an uneasy truce – who are barricaded into the all-but-abandoned and now-defunct police station that gives the film its title.

During one sequence in **From Dusk Till Dawn** this intertextuality is used as a joke, during a sequence in which one of the bar's patrons describes his experiences in Vietnam, during which he was the only survivor of his platoon and was forced to kill an entire regiment of NVA. However, rather than include the entire story, the film manipulates this cliché, drowning the words of the character out. His story is, after all, pure mimetic repetition, drawn up from the absurd dregs of a dozen B-movie war, horror, crime, and trash films. Similarly the characters, when faced with the knowledge of the vampires, are forced to consider their options for survival and all quote other horror films as sources of information. At these points the structure of generic convention itself becomes the source for humour between the director/scriptwriter and audience, who are all privileged to an extra-diagetic knowledge which the film's characters are not.

Actors – like genres – are familiar to an audience, maintaining their own particular signifying practice within the context of their cinematic appearances, and the metanarratives around their career. Audiences are familiar with the actors from their screen appearances and from the media articulation of that actor's image-as-personality. In **From Dusk Till Dawn**, which – despite its fake B-movie credentials – has an all-star cast (and a budget to match), the genre/s conventions are played simultaneously to the audience's expectations of the actors. Each actor in the film signifies their own relationship to cinema, and the audience's expectations of them. Juliette Lewis is cast in the role of a teenage girl, sexually naive but simultaneously seductively coy, she is, when faced with the vampires, able to fight and survive. She speaks in a generic-quasi-"white trash" (sic) Southern accent which is recognizable from her previous roles in the films **Kalifornia** (Dominic Sena, 1993) and **Natural Born Killers** (Oliver Stone, 1994), two films with which the audience are almost certainly familiar (her other film roles, whilst still important, slip from any direct metanarrative, her stardom is largely based on her portrayal of rebellious and/or "white trash" roles[3]). Similarly other actors within the film bring with them their own metanarratives; Quentin Tarantino, familiar from his appearances within his own heist/crime films,

notably (and perhaps wisely) understands his audience appeal and his character, Richie, dies as the movie switches genre from heist movie to horror. This is not to suggest that the metanarratives around Tarantino-as-actor would not sustain his appearance in a horror film, but that the death of Richie/exit of Tarantino helps to signify the change of pace of the film.

It is noticeable that many of the other actors within the film bring with them a cult status, inferring a degree of *hipness-by-osmosis* on the film. Thus Tom Savini – despite having only a handful of cameo appearances to his name – is famous for his special effects work on numerous horror films including **Night Of The Living Dead** (note also that Savini directed the 1990 remake of the film), a fact which fans of genre movies would certainly be familiar[4]. Fred Williamson, however brings an entirely different degree of cult-status with him; whilst Savini is famous for his horror work, Williamson is famous for his appearances primarily in blaxploitation and action movies: **Black Caeser** (1973), **Hell Up In Harlem** (1973), **Boss** (1974), **No Way Back** (1974), **Mean Johnny Barrows** (1975), **Fist Of Fear, Touch Of Death** (1977), **1990: The Bronx Warriors** (1983), **White Fire** (1983), and **Steele's Law** (1991), amongst many others. The casting of both of these cult actors – whose work is so familiar within specific genres – serves, in part, to position the film as a specific type of text.

The film also includes George Clooney in the cast, however, as a virtual unknown in cinema at the time of the film's release, he brings few

significations with him, other than his roles in the television series *ER* and in all-but-unseen B-grade movies **Return Of The Killer Tomatoes!** (John DeBello, 1988) and **Red Surf** (H Gordon Boos, 1990). Notably, following the release and success of the film Clooney won the MTV Movie Awards Breakthrough Performance Award, 1996. Note, also, that the fact that it was MTV which recognized the film, thus suggesting the twenty-something demographic of **From Dusk Till Dawn**'s audience. The film's other "unknown" actor is the youthful Ernest Liu.

The major star to appear in **From Dusk Till Dawn** is Harvey Keitel. In the film Keitel appears as Jacob, a faithless Minister, on a road trip with his family. As the film progresses so Keitel is forced to recognize the need for faith, and eventually dies in order that others can survive. His role is similar to those of religious figures in many other horror films, who – having lost their belief – find it again, but are destroyed in the process. Like the other actors within the film Keitel carries a signifying practice beyond the boundaries of the text. Primarily he is associated with portraying naturalistic figures – normally working class – in recognizable situations and locales. He is best known for his work with New York auteurs Martin Scorsese and Abel Ferrara, and has appeared in Scorsese's films **Who's That Knocking At My Door?** (1968), **Mean Streets** (1973), **Alice Doesn't Live Here Any More** (1974), **Taxi Driver** (1976), and **The Last Temptation Of Christ** (1988); and Ferrara's **Bad Lieutenant** (1992) and **Dangerous Game** (1993). Although not all specifically films dealing with crime, the frequently gritty narratives of these films certainly contain elements of borderline criminality, which undoubtedly assists in the perception of Keitel as a character actor versed in portraying suitably intense figures on the edges of society. As a consequence of this Keitel has appeared in various post-noir crime movies; **Order Of Death** (a.k.a. **Copkiller** a.k.a. **Corrupt**, Roberto Faenza, 1981), **The Two Jakes** (Jack Nicholson, 1990), **Point Of No Return** (1993, John Badham's remake of Luc Besson's 1991 film **La Femme Nikita**), as well as two films based on the live of mobster Bugsy Siegel: the television movie **The Virginia Hill Story** (Joel Schumacher, 1976), and **Bugsy** (Barry Levinson, 1991). Keitel's appearance in these films – thanks, primarily, to the metanarratives around his work – infers a degree of "authenticity", of "gritty realism", in these texts' representation/s of criminal life.

Keitel is also known for working with working with new and independent directors, and has appeared in **The Piano** (Jane Campion, 1993), **The Young Americans** (Danny Cannon, 1993), and **Reservoir Dogs**, as well as in "art-house" movies such as Theo Angelopoulos's **Ulysses' Gaze** (1995), Wayne Wang's slice-of-life **Smoke** (1995) and its companion piece **Blue In The Face** (directed by Wang and writer Paul Auster, 1995). Keitel has also been cast in films by Robert Altman and Spike Lee, appearing in Altman's

Buffalo Bill And The Indians (1976), and Lee's **Clockers** (1995). In these films Keitel again portrays naturalistic figures, many of who are characterized by an introspective intensity. If his appearances in "traditional" genre films are few, then Keitel's appearances in "fantastical" films are almost non-existent, there are a few exceptions; **Death Watch** (Bertrand Tavernier, 1980), **Saturn 3** (Stanley Donen, 1980), and **Two Evil Eyes** (George Romero and Dario Argento, 1990). None of which are particularly memorable films, and are hardly likely to inform the metatextual understanding of Keitel the audience would bring to a film such as **From Dusk Till Dawn**.

Jacob's role within the diagesis is defined by generic convention, confined to the straight jacket of a classic narrative form, in a mainstream film which does not deviate from convention beyond its superficially clever fusion of two apparently disparate genres. The audience are aware, from the introduction of Jacob as a faithless Minister onwards, that the genre demands that the character, having questioned his faith, will return to it when faced by the ultimate evil. Given that the role of Jacob is so clearly delineated, then, the casting of Keitel in the role would, on initial analysis, suggest a postmodern twist, or a camp gesture, but this is not the case, instead the narrative follows the expected formula. Keitel is thus rendered as unable to expand upon the role within the diagesis, and his position as a star is emptied of meaning because he no longer can be viewed as acting as a signifier for his own metanarrative. The scripting, action, direction and mise-en-scène prohibit any extension of the boundaries of the character. Indeed, even the appearance of the character is superficially anti-Keitel, who is hidden behind a beard and glasses. If Keitel signifies anything within **From Dusk Till Dawn**, it would be in the first section of the film, as the predominantly twenty-something demographic of the audience are familiar with Keitel primarily from his appearance in Tarantino's postmodern crime movies. However, whilst Tarantino's role ends as the "horror" genre section of the film begins, Keitel's character only really "makes sense" within the second section of the film (there is, after all, little need for a faithless minister consumed by existential nausea in a heist movie); as such Keitel's character only emerges to fulfil his function within the second part of the film. However, the further Jacob emerges, the further Keitel-as-recognisable-signifier vanishes, disappearing behind generic convention, his star personality becoming as translucent as the celluloid projection on the screen.

Finally then, **From Dusk Till Dawn** exists as a genre movie, which, despite being lavishly produced is merely a high budget B-movie. Whilst many stars can emerge through repeated roles in such films, Keitel is able to vanish. In a medium in which stardom and recognition are validated as the highest marks of success, then to disappear into the text, to submit to narrative, to suspend personality, is a radical gesture, the gesture of an actor.

NOTES

1. The innocent girl who survives because of her virginity is one of the central themes of splatter movies; for further reading see Carol Clover's book *Men Women And Chainsaws*, BFI, 1995.

2. See, for example, Tarantino's script for **Natural Born Killers** with its references to cinematic texts such as Terrence Malick's **Badlands** (1974), as well as stylistic references to MTV. Whilst Tarantino's directorial debut, **Reservoir Dogs**, makes narrative references to Ringo Lam's **City On Fire** (1987), and stylistic nods to films by Sam Peckinpah amongst others.

3. Juliette Lewis has appeared in this rebellious guise in **Strange Days** (Kathryn Bigelow, 1995) and – to a lesser degree – **What's Eating Gilbert Grape?** (Lasse Hallstrom, 1993), while her naive sexuality became the focus of a key sequence in Martin Scorsese's remake of **Cape Fear** (1991).

4. One key element of fandom is the fanzine, and horror film audiences are more than catered for by magazines such as *Fangoria*, which focus at length on the verisimilitude of special effects.

A HARVEY KEITEL FILMOGRAPHY

Who's That Knocking At My Door? (1968)
Mean Streets (1973)
Pueblo (1973, TV)
Alice Doesn't Live Here Anymore (1974)
The Virginia Hill Story (1974, TV)
Shining Star (1975, *aka* That's The Way Of The World)
Taxi Driver (1976)
Buffalo Bill And The Indians (1976)
Mother, Jugs & Speed (1976)
The Duellists (1977)
Welcome To L.A. (1977)
Fingers (1978)
Blue Collar (1978)
Eagle's Wing (1979)
Bad Timing (1980)
La Mort En Direct (1980, *aka* Deathwatch)
Saturn 3 (1980)
The Border (1982)
La Nuit De Varennes (1982)
Exposed (1983)
Copkiller (1983, *aka* Corrupt *aka* Order Of Death)
Une Pierre Dans La Bouche (1983)
Nemo (1984, *aka* Dream One)
Falling In Love (1984)
The Knight Of The Dragon (1985)
Un Complicato Intrigo Di Donne, Vicoli E Delitti (1986, *aka* Camorra)
Blindside (1986)
The Men's Club (1986)
Off Beat (1986)
Wise Guys (1986)
The Pick-up Artist (1987)
Dear America: Letters Home From Vietnam (1987)
Down Where The Buffalo Go (1987)
L'Inchiesta (1987, *aka* The Inquiry)
The Last Temptation Of Christ (1988)
Caro Gorbaciov (1988)
Grandi Cacciatori (1988, *aka* White Hunter)
January Man (1989)

The Two Jakes (1990)
La Batalla De Los Tres Reyes (1990)
Play Dead (1990)
Two Evil Eyes (1990)
Mortal Thoughts (1991)
Thelma And Louise (1991)
Bugsy (1991)
Sister Act (1992)
Reservoir Dogs (1992)
Bad Lieutenant (1992)
Dangerous Game (1993, *aka* **Snake Eyes**)
Rising Sun (1993)
Point Of No Return (1993, *aka* **The Assassin**)
The Piano (1993)
The Young Americans (1993)
Pulp Fiction (1994)
Monkey Trouble (1994)
Imaginary Crimes (1994)
Somebody To Love (1994)
Who Do You Think You're Fooling? (1994)
Get Shorty (1995)
Clockers (1995)
Smoke (1995)
Blue In The Face (1995)
Ulysses' Gaze (1995)
Head Above Water (1996)
From Dusk Till Dawn (1996)
Cop Land (1997)
City Of Industry (1997)
FairyTale: A True Story (1997)
Full Tilt Boogie (1997)
My West (1998)
Lulu On The Bridge (1998)
Finding Graceland (1998)
Jack Sheppard And Jonathan Wild: A Tale Of Old London (1998)
Shadrach (1998)
Three Seasons (1998)
Holy Smoke (1999)
An Interesting State (1999)
Prince Of Central Park (1999)
U-571 (1999)

INDEX OF FILMS

Page number in bold indicates an illustration

DENNIS HOPPER *Jack Hunter (editor)*
MOVIE TOP TEN

DENNIS HOPPER One of the most talented but controversial actors of recent decades, almost as notorious for his off-screen hell-raising as he is for his roles in such powerful films as his self-directed **The Last Movie**, David Lynch's **Blue Velvet**, and Tim Hunter's **River's Edge**.

Jack Hunter (author of film studies *Inside Teradome* and *Eros In Hell*) has selected his own chronological Top Ten of Dennis Hopper's movies, which are analysed in illustrated, in-depth essays by some of the best cutting-edge film critics of today. The result is both an incisive overview of Dennis Hopper as an actor, and an anthology of films by some of the leading cult directors of recent decades such as Wim Wenders, Tobe Hooper, David Lynch, Tim Hunter, Henry Jaglom, Curtis Harrington, and Hopper himself.

Featured films include: **Night Tide, The Last Movie, Tracks, Speed, The American Friend, Out Of The Blue, Texas Chainsaw Massacre 2, Blue Velvet, Rivers Edge**, and **Paris Trout**.

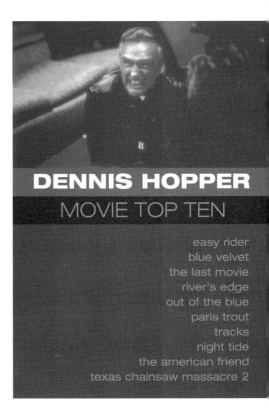

DENNIS HOPPER
MOVIE TOP TEN

easy rider
blue velvet
the last movie
river's edge
out of the blue
paris trout
tracks
night tide
the american friend
texas chainsaw massacre 2

CINEMA   Trade paperback   1 871592 86 0   192 pages   169mm x 244mm   £12.95

HARVEY KEITEL *Jack Hunter (editor)*
MOVIE TOP TEN

HARVEY KEITEL One of the most versatile and acclaimed actors of recent years, always willing to take on new, challenging roles ranging from the dissolute cop in Abel Ferrara's **Bad Lieutenant** and trigger-happy robber in Tarantino's **Reservoir Dogs**, to the taciturn settler in Jane Campion's **The Piano**.

Jack Hunter (author of film studies *Inside Teradome* and *Eros In Hell*) has selected his own chronological Top Ten of Harvey Keitel's movies, which are analysed in illustrated, in-depth essays by some of the best cutting-edge film critics of today. The result is both an incisive overview of Harvey Keitel as an actor, and an anthology of films by some of the leading cult directors of recent years, including Quentin Tarantino, Martin Scorsese, Nic Roeg, Abel Ferrara, Spike Lee, James Toback, and Jane Campion.

Featured films include: **Fingers, Mean Streets, Cop Killer, Bad Timing, Bad Lieutenant, Dangerous Game, Reservoir Dogs, The Piano, From Dusk Til Dawn**, and **Clockers**.

HARVEY KEITEL
MOVIE TOP TEN

fingers
mean streets
cop killer
bad timing
dangerous game
reservoir dogs
bad lieutenant
the piano
from dusk 'til dawn
clockers

CINEMA   Trade paperback   1 871592 87 9   192 pages   169mm x 244mm   £12.95

CREATION BOOKS

ROBERT DE NIRO *Jack Hunter (editor)*
MOVIE TOP TEN

ROBERT DE NIRO. One of the most versatile and acclaimed actors of recent years, famous for the uncompromising method approach he brings to roles ranging from the psychotic Travis Bickle in Martin Scorsese's seminal **Taxi Driver**, to the nerveless robber of Michael Mann's **Heat** and the loser in Tarantino's **Jackie Brown**.

Series editor Jack Hunter has selected his own chronological Top Ten of Robert De Niro's movies, which are analysed in illustrated, in-depth essays by some of the best cutting-edge film critics of today.

The result is both an incisive overview of Robert De Niro as an actor, and an anthology of films by some of the leading directors of recent decades such as Martin Scorsese, Michael Mann, Quentin Tarantino, Sergio Leone, Bernardo Bertolucci, and Francis Ford Coppola.

Featured films include: **Taxi Driver, Raging Bull, Angel Heart, Once Upon a Time In America, Jackie Brown, King of Comedy, Heat, 1900, Cape Fear,** and **Godfather II.**

CINEMA   Trade paperback   1 871592 88 7   192 pages   169mm x 244mm   £12.95

JOHNNY DEPP *Jack Hunter (editor)*
MOVIE TOP TEN

JOHNNY DEPP. One of the most enigmatic and uncompromising actors of recent years, famous for a wide variety of movies ranging from Tim Burton's gothic fable **Edward Scissorhands** and lurid pulp movie tribute **Ed Wood**, to Terry Gilliam's psychedelic, paranoiac drug epic **Fear And Loathing**.

Series editor Jack Hunter has selected his own chronological Top Ten of Johnny Depp's movies, which are analysed in illustrated, in-depth essays by some of the best cutting-edge film critics of today. The result is both an incisive overview of Johnny Depp as an actor, and an anthology of films by some of the leading cult directors of recent decades such as Tim Burton, Jim Jarmusch, Terry Gilliam, John Waters, and Wes Craven.

Featured films include: **Edward Scissorhands, Donnie Brasco, Ed Wood, Cry-Baby, Fear And Loathing In Las Vegas, What's Eating Gilbert Grape, Nightmare On Elm Street, Platoon, Nick Of Time,** and **Dead Man.**

CINEMA   Trade paperback   1 871592 89 5   192 pages   169mm x 244mm   £12.95

CREATION BOOKS

① KILLING FOR CULTURE

Kerekes & Slater

Killing For Culture is a definitive investigation into the urban myth of the "snuff movie". Includes: FEATURE FILM – from *Peeping Tom* to *Videodrome* and beyond; MONDO FILM – from *Mondo Cane* to present day 'shockumentaries'; DEATH FILM – from *Faces Of Death* to real deaths captured on film such as live-TV suicides, executions, and news footage.

Illustrated by stunning photographs from cinema, documentary and real life, **Killing For Culture** is a necessary book which examines and questions the human obsession with images of violence, dismemberment and death, and the way our society is coping with an increased profusion of these disturbing yet compelling images from all quarters. Includes filmography and index.

"Well-researched and highly readable, Killing For Culture *is a must-have."*
— FILM THREAT

CINEMA/CULTURE   Trade Paperback   1 871592 20 8   169 x 244mm   288 pages   £14.95

② INSIDE TERADOME

Jack Hunter

Freakshows – human anomalies presented for spectacle – have flourished throughout recorded history. The birth of the movies provided a further outlet for these displays, which in turn led to a peculiar strain of bizarre cinema: Freak Film. **Inside Teradome** is a comprehensive, fully illustrated guide to the roots and development of this fascinating, often disturbing cinematic genre.

Including: Teratology: freaks in myth and medicine; the history of freakshows, origins of cinema; influence of sideshows on cinema; use of human anomalies in cinema; freaks and geeks; bizarre cinema: mutilation and other fetishes; illustrated filmography; index; over 350 photographs. From the real-life grotesqueries of Tod Browning's *Freaks*, to the modern nightmare vision of *Santa Sangre*, **Inside Teradome** reveals a twisted thread of voyeuristic sickness running both through cinema and the society it mirrors.

CINEMA/CULTURE   Trade Paperback   1 871592 41 0   169 x 244mm   256 pages   £14.95

③ DEATHTRIPPING

Jack Sargeant

Deathtripping is an illustrated history, account and critique of the "Cinema Of Transgression", providing a long-overdue and comprehensive documentation of this essential modern sub-cultural movement. Including: A brief history of underground/trash cinema: seminal influences including Andy Warhol, Jack Smith, George and Mike Kuchar, John Waters. Interviews with key film-makers, including Richard Kern, Nick Zedd, Cassandra Stark, Beth B, Tommy Turner; plus associates such as Joe Coleman, Lydia Lunch, Lung Leg and David Wojnarowicz Notes and essays on transgressive cinema, philosophy of transgression; manifestos, screenplays; film index and bibliography.

Heavily illustrated with rare and sometimes disturbing photographs, **Deathtripping** is a unique guide to a style of film-making whose impact and influence can no longer be ignored.

CINEMA/CULTURE   Trade Paperback   1 871592 29 1   169 x 244mm   256 pages   £14.95

④ FRAGMENTS OF FEAR

Andy Boot

Fragments Of Fear is an illustrated history of an often neglected film genre: the British Horror Movie. The book examines a wide range of British horror films, and the stories behind them, from the early melodramas of Tod Slaughter right through to Hammer and their rivals Tigon and Amicus, plus mavericks like Michael Reeves, sex/horror director Peter Walker and more recent talents such as Clive Barker, director of *Hellraiser*. Films discussed range in scope from the sadism of *Peeping Tom* to the mutant SF of *A Clockwork Orange* and the softcore porn/horror of Jose Larraz' *Vampyres*.

With plentiful illustrations, author Andy Boot unravels a tangled history and discovers many little-known gems amid the more familiar images of Hammer, including a wealth of exploitational cinema, to establish the British horror movie as a genre which can easily stand up to its more lauded American counterpart in the depth and diversity of its scope.

CINEMA   Trade Paperback   1 871592 35 6   169 x 244mm   288 pages   £14.95

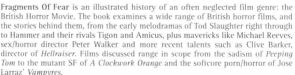

CREATION BOOKS

⑤ DESPERATE VISIONS   *Jack Stevenson*

John Waters is the notorious director of *Pink Flamingos, Female Trouble, Desperate Living* and *Hairspray*, amongst other cult movie classics.

    Desperate Visions features several in-depth interviews with Waters, as well as with members of his legendary entourage including Divine, Mary Vivian Pearce, Mink Stole and Miss Jean Hill. George & Mike Kuchar are the directors of such low-budget/underground classics as *Sins Of The Fleshapoids* and *Hold Me While I'm Naked*. Their visionary trash aesthetic was a great influence on the young John Waters.

    Desperate Visions includes extensive interviews with the Kuchars, as well as a comprehensive assessment of their career and influence. Also included is a unique feature on actress Marion Eaton, star of the gothic porn epic *Thundercrack!*.

    With many rare photographs, filmography and index, **Desperate Visions** is an essential introduction to the wild world of John Waters, and to the outrageous camp/underground film tradition which his movies exemplify.

CINEMA/CULTURE Trade Paperback 1 871592 34 8   169 x 244mm   256 pages   £14.95

⑥ THE NAKED LENS   *Jack Sargeant*

The Naked Lens is a vital collection of essays and interviews focusing on the most significant interfaces between the Beat writers, Beat culture and cinema; films by, featuring, or inspired by: WILLIAM S BURROUGHS • ALLEN GINSBERG • JACK KEROUAC • CHARLES BUKOWSKI • BRION GYSIN ANTHONY BALCH • RON RICE JOHN CASSAVETES • ANDY WARHOL • BOB DYLAN • KLAUS MAECK • GUS VAN SANT *& many others*

    Including interviews with writers such as Allen Ginsberg, directors such as Robert Frank and actors such as Taylor Mead; plus detailed examination of key Beat texts and cult classics such as *Pull My Daisy, Chappaqua, Towers Open Fire* and *The Flower Thief*; verité and performance films such as *Shadows, Don't Look Back* and *Wholly Communion*; B-movies such as *The Subterraneans, Beat Generation* and Roger Corman's *Bucket Of Blood*; and Hollywood-style adaptations from *Heart Beat* and *Barfly* through to Cronenberg's *Naked Lunch*.

CINEMA/BEAT CULTURE Trade Paperback 1 871592 67 4   169 x 244mm   288 pages   £12.95

⑦ HOUSE OF HORROR   *Jack Hunter*

HAMMER FILMS remains one of the most successful and legendary of all British film companies. Their name is synonymous with gothic horror throughout the world.

    House Of Horror traces the complete history of Hammer, from its early origins through to its golden era of classic horror movies, and presents a comprehensive overview of Hammer's importance and influence in world cinema.

    House Of Horror includes interviews with Hammer stars Christopher Lee and Peter Cushing, detailed analysis of all Hammer's horror and fantasy films and their key directors, and dozens of rare and exciting photographs and posters; plus a fully illustrated A–Z of key Hammer personnel from both sides of the camera, a directory of unfilmed projects, a complete filmography, and full film index.

    Third, expanded edition

CINEMA Trade Paperback 1 871592 19 4   169 x 244mm   224 pages   £12.95

⑧ MEAT IS MURDER!   *Mikita Brottman*

Violent death, murder, mutilation, eating and defaecation, ritualism, bodily extremes; cannibalism combines these crucial themes to represent one of the most symbolically charged narratives in the human psychic repertoire.

    As a grotesque figure of power, threat, and atavistic appetites, the cannibal has played a formidable role in the tales told by members of all cultures – whether oral, written, or filmic – and embodies the ultimate extent of transgressive behaviour to which human beings can be driven.

    Meat Is Murder! is a unique and explicit exploration of the stories that are told about cannibals, from classical myth to contemporary film and fiction, and features an in-depth illustrated critique of cannibalism as portrayed in the cinema, from mondo and exploitation films to horror movies and arthouse classics. It also details the atrocious crimes of real life cannibals of the modern age, such as Albert Fish, Ed Gein, Jeffrey Dahmer and Andrei Chikatilo.

CINEMA/CULTURE   Trade Paperback   1 871592 90 9   169 x 244mm   208 pages   £14.95

⑨ EROS IN HELL

Jack Hunter

SEX: The history of "pink" movies, from *Daydream* to *Ai No Corrida* and beyond, including the pop avant-garde violence of Koji Wakamatsu films such as *Violated Angels* and *Violent Virgin*. Bondage and S/M from *Moju* to *Captured For Sex* and Kinbiken rope torture.

BLOOD: From *Shogun Assassin* and *Psycho Junkie* to the killing orgies of *Guinea Pig* and *Atrocity*; from the "pink horror" nightmare *Entrails Of A Virgin* to the post-punk yakuza bloodbaths of Kei Fujiwara's *Organ* and Takashi Miike's *Fudoh*.

MADNESS: Homicidal psychosis, hallucination, mutation: *Tetsuo*, *Death Powder*, the films of Shozin Fukui such as *Pinocchio 964* and *Rubber's Lover*. Post-punk excess, nihilism, violence, suicide: *Labyrinth Of Dreams*, *Squareworld*, *Tokyo Crash*.

Eros In Hell examines all these movies and many more besides, is profusely illustrated with rare and unusual photographs, comprising a unique guide to the most prolific, fascinating and controversial underground/alternative cinema in the world.

CINEMA Trade paperback 1 871592 93 3 169 x 244 mm 256 pages £14.95

⑩ CHARLIE'S FAMILY

Jim VanBebber

Charles Manson and The Family. The Love and Terror Cult. The Dune Buggy Attack Battalion. Devil's Witches, Devil's Hole. Jim Van Bebber's mind-blowing movie **Charlie's Family** is the most accurate and uncompromising cinematic portrayal of the exterminating angels of Death Valley '69, a psychotic assault of sex, drugs and violence that propels the viewer headlong into the Manson experience.

Charlie's Family reconstructs the cataclysms of creepy-crawl and the Tate/La Bianca murders in vivid relief, showing us not only a devastating acid blood orgy but also the ways in which one man's messianic power held sway over an entire killer korps of sexually submissive yet homicidal believers.

The illustrated screenplay of **Charlie's Family** contains nearly 100 amazing photographs, including 16 in full colour, as well as the complete script and 16 original storyboards. It also includes the definitive illustrated essay on Manson-related movies, written by Jim Morton, main contributor to *Incredibly Strange Films*, as well as an introduction by esteemed underground film critic Jack Sargeant.

CINEMA/TRUE CRIME Trade paperback 1 871592 94 1 169 x 244 mm 192 pages £14.95

⑪ RENEGADE SISTERS

Bev Zalcock

From boarding school to women's prison, biker packs to urban vigilantes, rampaging girl gangs have long been a staple feature of exploitation/independent cinema.

Renegade Sisters examines the whole history of girl gangs on film, focusing on B-classics like Russ Meyer's *Faster, Pussycat! Kill! Kill!*, Herschell Gordon Lewis' *She-Devils On Wheels*, and Jack Hill's *Switchblade Sisters*; Women-In-Prison movies such as Stephanie Rothman's *Terminal Island* and Jack Hill's *Big Doll House*, with Pam Grier; camp SF like *Cat Women Of The Moon* and *Queen Of Outer Space*; plus many other deviant displays of girl power from various genres, right through to Todd Morris and Deborah Twiss' ferocious, post-Tarantino *A Gun For Jennifer*.

Renegade Sisters also looks at Queercore girls; the feminist/lesbian movies of Barbara Hammer, Jennifer Reeder, Anie Stanley and others, and includes interviews with film makers Vivienne Dick and Julie Jenkins, as well as *A Gun For Jennifer* writer/producer Deborah Twiss. With dozens of photographic illustrations.

CINEMA/WOMEN'S STUDIES Trade paperback 1 871592 92 5 169 x 244 mm 208 pages £14.95

⑫ BABYLON BLUE

David Flint

Filmed erotica and adult entertainment has finally come of age. Porn has at last become something that can be increasingly freely and openly enjoyed, and celebrated as a specialist leisure activity in its own right, with its own history and critical lineage. Despite decades of resistance, the long-established hardcore porn production houses have built an alternative film industry, complete with its own visionaries, superstars and standard-bearers.

Babylon Blue examines the '60s roots of global modern-day erotic cinema – from naturist films to the "nudie-cuties" of Russ Meyer – through to various incarnations of Euro-porn and hardcore, charting the rise, decline and resurrection of the genre since the early '70s. Finally, author David Flint expertly chronicles the so-called New Porn Generation – the New Wave of adult movies, as epitomised by the stylish and sophisticated films of Andrew Blake, Michael Ninn and the Dark Brothers.

Visually loaded with profuse and daring illustrations, **Babylon Blue** is the last word on sex cinema, featuring profiles of key directors, producers and performers, and detailed critiques of the finest adult movies of all time.

CINEMA/CULTURE Trade paperback 1 84068 002 4 256 pages 169 x 244mm £16.95

13 HOLLYWOOD HEX   *Mikita Brottman*

From the myths of old Hollywood to recent on-screen accidents, the motion picture industry has long been associated with violent and untimely death. Hollywood has always been a magnet for suicides, murders, mysterious accidents and brutal mayhem; the simple fact is that, in the age of motion pictures, human death has become an inescapable part of show business. **Hollywood Hex** is a study of films that have, in one way or another, resulted in death and destruction. Some are directly responsible for the accidental deaths of those involved in their creation; others have caused tragedy indirectly by inspiring occult movements, serial killers, copycat crimes, psychotic behavior in audiences, or bizarre and freakish coincidences. These "cursed" films include *The Exorcist, Rosemary's Baby, Twilight Zone – The Movie* and *The Crow*; films that have become notorious and compelling in their new role as inadvertent epitaphs, as documents on the subject of human mortality.

The book contains interviews with sexploitation producer David Friedman, screenwriter Antonio Passolini, director Lindsay Honey and porn actress/producer Jane Hamilton, and includes a stunning eight-page full-colour section.

CINEMA/CULTURE   Trade paperback 1 871592 85 2   256 pages   169 x 244mm   £14.95

DEATH AND DESTINY IN THE DREAM FACTORY
AN ILLUSTRATED HISTORY OF CURSED MOVIES

14 LOST HIGHWAYS *Jack Sargeant & Stephanie Watson*

The road movie: a complex cinematic journey that incorporates mythic themes of questing and searching, the need for being, for love, for a home and for a promise of a different future, and yet also serves as a map of current cultural desires, dreams, and fears.

Lost Highways explores the history of the road movie through a series of detailed essays on key films within the genre. Through these comprehensive and absorbing studies a clear and concise post-modern picture of the road movie emerges, tracing hitherto neglected intersections with other genres such as the western, film noir, horror, and even science fiction.

From *The Wizard Of Oz* to *Crash, Apocalypse Now* to *Vanishing Point, The Wild Bunch* to *Easy Rider*, **Lost Highways** is the definitive illustrated guide to a diverse body of film which holds at its nucleus the quintessential cinematic/cultural interchange of modern times.

Jack Sargeant is an acclaimed underground film critic, and is the author of Deathtripping and Naked Lens.

AN ILLUSTRATED HISTORY OF ROAD MOVIES
Jack Sargeant & Stephanie Watson

CINEMA/CULTURE   Trade paperback 1 871592 68 2   256 pages   169mm x 244mm   £14.95

15 A TASTE OF BLOOD   *Christopher Wayne Curry*

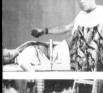

The incredibly popular, violent horror films of recent decades, such as *Texas Chainsaw Massacre, Friday The 13th*, and *A Nightmare On Elm Street*, owe much of their existence to the undisputed Godfather of Gore – Herschell Gordon Lewis. In 1963 Lewis, with his monumental splatter movie Blood Feast, single-handedly changed the face of horror cinema forever.

As well as virtually inventing the gore genre, Lewis also produced a number of nudie and roughie movies, as well as sampling the full gamut of exploitation subjects ranging from wife-swapping and ESP to rock'n'roll and LSD. **A Taste Of Blood** details all these, plus gore classics such as *2,000 Maniacs, Gore-Gore Girls, Color Me Blood Red* and *Wizard Of Gore*, placing them in context amid the roots and development of the exploitation film.

A Taste Of Blood is a definitive study which not only chronicles Lewis' career as the master of exploitation, but also contains interviews with him and many of his former collaborators, including David F Friedman, Bill Rogers, Daniel Krogh, Mal Arnold and Hedda Lubin. These are interwoven with commentary, extremely rare photographs, ad mats, production stills, posters, and a thorough synopsis of each of Lewis' three dozen influential films. Also included is a stunning 8-page colour section of graphic screen gore.

THE FILMS OF
HERSCHELL GORDON LEWIS

CINEMA   Trade paperback 1 871592 91 7   256 pages   169mm x 244mm   £16.95

NECRONOMICON 1

Andy Black (ed)

Necronomicon Book One continues the singular, thought-provoking exploration of transgressive cinema begun by the much-respected and acclaimed magazine of the same name. The transition to annual book format has allowed for even greater depth and diversity within the journal's trademarks of progressive critique and striking photographic content.

Including: MARCO FERRERI • TEXAS CHAINSAW MASSACRE • BARBARA STEELE • FRIGHTMARE • JEAN ROLLIN • DEEP THROAT • DARIO ARGENTO LAST TANGO IN PARIS • H P LOVECRAFT • WITCHFINDER GENERAL HERSCHELL GORDON LEWIS • EVIL DEAD • ABEL FERRARA *and much more*

CINEMA   Trade Paperback   1 871592 37 2   169 x 244mm   192 pages   £12.95

NECRONOMICON 2

Andy Black (ed)

Book Two of the journal of horror and erotic cinema, continuing the thought-provoking exploration of transgressive film making begun by the first volume. With more illustrated insights into the world of celluloid sex and violence, including:

JESUS FRANCO • SADEAN CINEMA • RUSS MEYER MANSON, POLANSKI, MACBETH • NEW JAPANESE PORNO GEORGE A ROMERO • SS EXPLOITATION • BABA YAGA/CEMETERY MAN WALERIAN BOROWCZYK • DARIO ARGENTO • FEMALE VAMPIRES • SE7EN *and much more*

"Lovingly produced and amply illustrated... engaging... Heady stuff."
—Sight & Sound

CINEMA   Trade paperback   1 871592 38 2   169 x 244mm   192 pages   £12.95

MAIL ORDER FORM
(please photocopy if you do not wish to cut up your book)

TITLE (please tick box)	PRICE(UK)	PRICE(US)	QTY
☐ Dennis Hopper Movie Top 10	£12.95	$17.95	
☐ Harvey Keitel Movie Top 10	£12.95	$17.95	
☐ Robert De Niro Movie Top 10	£12.95	$17.95	
☐ Johnny Depp Movie Top 10	£12.95	$17.95	
☐ Killing for Culture	£14.95	$19.95	
☐ Inside Teradome	£14.95	$19.95	
☐ Deathtripping	£14.95	$19.95	
☐ Fragments of Fear	£14.95	$19.95	
☐ Desperate Visions	£14.95	$19.95	
☐ The Naked Lens	£12.95	$19.95	
☐ House of Horror	£12.95	$19.95	
☐ Meat Is Murder!	£14.95	$19.95	
☐ Eros In Hell	£14.95	$19.95	
☐ Charlie's Family	£11.95	$10.95	
☐ Renegade Sisters	£14.95	$19.95	
☐ Babylon Blue	£16.95	$22.95	
☐ Hollywood Hex	£14.95	$19.95	
☐ A Taste of Blood	£16.95	$22.95	
☐ Lost Highways	£14.95	$19.95	
☐ Necronomicon 1	£12.95	$17.95	
☐ Necronomicon 2	£12.95	$17.95	

SUBTOTAL ....

P&P ....

TOTAL ....

☐ I enclose cheque/money order/cash

☐ I wish to pay by ☐ Visa ☐ Mastercard

Card No:

Expiry Date _____

Signature _____ Date _____

Name_____

Address_____

_____

_____

UK: Add 10% to total price for p&p. EUROPE: Add 15%. Payment with order to: Creation Books, 83 Clerkenwell Road. London EC1R 5AR (£sterling US: Add 10% to total price for p&p. REST OF THE WORLD: Add 20%. Payment with order to: Creation Books, PO Box 13512, Berkeley, CA 94712 (US$ or order direct from our Website at: www.creationbooks.com

CREATION BOOKS